SIMPLE THAI COO

KEN HOM

SIMPLE THAI COOKERY

KEN HOM

Step by step to
everyone's favourite
Thai recipes

BOOKS

About the author

Ken Hom is widely regarded as one the world's greatest authorities on Oriental cooking. He has made several series for the BBC including *Hot Wok*, *Travels with a Hot Wok* and *Foolproof Chinese Cookery*, and his many books are worldwide bestsellers. He is a consultant to Noble House Leisure Limited, which includes the Yellow River Cafés and other restaurants, and lives in London, Paris, south-west France and Bangkok.

Dedication

Once again to Kurt and Penny Wachtveitl and Norbert Kostner, as well as all the staff at the Oriental in Bangkok.

Food photography by Jean Cazals

Published by BBC Books,
BBC Worldwide Ltd,
Woodlands,
80 Wood Lane,
London W12 0TT

First published in hardback as *Foolproof Thai Cookery* in 2002
This paperback edition first published in 2006
Copyright © Promo Group Ltd 2002
The moral right of Ken Hom to be identified as the author of this work has been asserted.

Food photography © Jean Cazals 2002

ISBN 0 563 49328 3

Commissioning editor: Vivien Bowler
Project editor: Sarah Lavelle
Copy editor: Jane Middleton
Art direction and design: Lisa Pettibone
Production controller: Susan Currie
Home economist: Marie Ange Lapierre
Stylist: Sue Rowlands

The publishers would like to thank the following for supplying items used in the photographs: Kara Kara, William Levene and Divertimenti.

Set in Univers
Printed and bound in Italy by Printer Trento Srl
Colour separations by Kestrel Digital Colour, Chelmsford

Contents

Introduction

I have been visiting Thailand for decades and have grown to love its people, the land, the culture and especially the delightful and glorious cuisine. I remember my first taste of Thai food, exploding with spices and herbs in combinations I had never imagined. Since then I have sampled and feasted my way through many colourful food markets, restaurants and home kitchens throughout Thailand. I continue to be amazed at the ability of Thai cooks to offer creative variations on familiar ingredients.

I was fortunate enough to work for a number of years at that famous Bangkok landmark, the Oriental Hotel. Thanks to Kurt Wachtveitl, general manager *par excellence*, I was given the opportunity to study Thai cookery by working with the greatest contemporary masters of that noble tradition. It was there that I learned the fundamentals of Thai cooking techniques, ingredients, flavours and harmonies. I attended classes at the well-known Thai Cooking School and worked alongside and under the supervision of Norbert Kostner, executive chef at the Oriental. Norbert is married to a Thai, speaks fluent Thai and, having lived in Thailand for decades, is a true convert to Thai culture. Most important, he is an outstanding exponent of Thai cuisine. His knowledge of all cookery traditions is prodigious but his first love is for the Thai. Norbert was kind enough to take me under his wing and share with me all his knowledge of and veneration for the cuisine of his adopted land.

His enthusiasm for Thai cookery inspired me to emulate him and to make Thai traditions my own. My experience at the Oriental deepened my appreciation of Thai cuisine and brought me to love the surprising and delicious combinations of tastes and textures that characterize that remarkable tradition. Ever since, I have used Thai flavours in my everyday cooking, whether it be classic Chinese, French or, most often, 'fusion' style. I have noted that every culinary tradition has gained from this mixture of Thai influences.

My hope is that you will use this book as a handy and helpful guide to the increasingly popular cuisine of Thailand and that you will find, as I have, how wonderful, refreshing and easy Thai cookery can be.

I remember my first taste of Thai food, exploding with spices and herbs in combinations I had never imagined.

Ingredients and Equipment

INGREDIENTS

It has taken just a few decades for Thai food, with its unique ingredients, to win popularity with home cooks and master chefs alike. Thai ingredients have become a valued staple in the pantries of both home and restaurant kitchens. This is partly in response to healthy eating concerns – most Thai cooking is light and clean, with little added animal fat such as butter, cream or cheese. Furthermore, with global connections now commonplace, many formerly exotic Thai ingredients have become familiar and readily available. And as Thai immigration has expanded throughout the West, its cooking has become cross-pollinated with that of other cultures.

Below is a brief guide to Thai ingredients used in this book.

Aubergines, Chinese

In Thailand there are several types of aubergine, ranging from ones that look like large, green peas to long, green varieties that resemble bananas. Some are even eaten raw, with a sauce or dip. Chinese aubergines are pleasing, purple-skinned vegetables ranging in size from the large, plump ones found in all supermarkets and greengrocers to the small, thin variety that the Thais (and the Chinese) prefer for their more delicate flavour.

Choose aubergines with smooth, unblemished skin. Thai chefs do not normally peel aubergines, since the skin preserves their texture, taste and shape. Large Western-style aubergines should be cut according to the recipe, sprinkled with a little salt and left to drain for 20 minutes. They should then be rinsed and any liquid blotted dry with kitchen paper. This process extracts the bitter juices and excess moisture before cooking, giving a truer taste to a dish. The aubergines retain their own virtues while blending in with the other ingredients. This procedure is unnecessary if you are using Chinese aubergines.

Basil

Basil and many other fresh, aromatic herbs are used in Thai cookery, to flavour salads, curries and stir-fries. There are three types of Thai basil, of which the most common has small, intense dark-green leaves with a purple-red tinge. It is extremely fragrant, with a deep anise scent. Thai basil is widely available in Asian food shops but Mediterranean-style basil makes an acceptable substitute.

Chillies

Chillies are the seed pods of capsicum plants and can be obtained fresh, dried or ground.

Above: three varieties of aubergine

They come in many colours, hundreds of varieties and varying degrees of intensity (heat) but the commercially available ones are few in number and one readily learns which are which and how to use them. Thais are said to use chillies with almost reckless abandon, but beginners should be more circumspect. It is perhaps best to begin 'cool' and gradually increase the heat. The seeds are the source of most of the heat. Removing them reduces the intensity but leaves much rich flavour.

Fresh chillies

Fresh chillies should look fresh and bright with no brown patches or black spots. Red chillies are generally milder than green ones because they sweeten as they ripen. The small red or green Thai chillies are especially pungent, and can be fierily hot.

To prepare fresh chillies, rinse them under cold water, then slit them lengthways with a small, sharp knife. Remove and discard the seeds. Rinse the chillies again under cold running water, then prepare them according to the recipe. Wash your hands, knife and chopping board before preparing other foods, and be careful not to touch your eyes until you have washed your hands thoroughly.

Dried red chillies

The dried red chillies used in Thailand are small, thin and about 1 cm (½ in) long. They are normally left whole or cut in half lengthways with the seeds left in and used to season oil for stir-fried dishes, sauces, and braises.

Dried chillies can be found in Thai and Chinese food shops, as well as in most supermarkets. They will keep indefinitely in a tightly covered jar.

Chilli oil/chilli dipping sauce

Chilli oil is used throughout Southeast Asia as a dipping condiment as well as a seasoning. It varies in strength according to the chillies used. The Thai and Malaysian ones are especially hot, while the Taiwanese and Chinese versions are more subtle.

Commercial chilli oils are quite acceptable but the home-made version is best, so I have included a recipe below. Remember that chilli oil is too intense to be used as the sole cooking oil; it is best combined with milder oils.

Clockwise from left: dried red chillies, fresh red chillies, chilli oil

This recipe includes pepper and black beans for additional flavours so that it can also be used as a dipping sauce.

150 ml (5 fl oz) groundnut oil
2 tablespoons chopped dried red chillies
1 tablespoon Sichuan peppercorns
2 tablespoons whole salted black beans

Heat a wok or large frying-pan over a high heat, then add the oil, followed by all the rest of the ingredients. Cook over a low heat for about 10 minutes, then remove from the heat and leave to cool. Pour into a jar and leave for 2 days, then strain the oil. Store in a tightly sealed glass jar in a cool, dark place, where it will keep indefinitely.

Chilli powder

Chilli powder, also known as cayenne pepper, is made from dried red chillies and is extremely pungent. As with chillies in general, your own palate will determine the acceptable degree of heat for each dish when adding chilli powder. 'Use sparingly' are the watchwords for beginners.

Left to right: winged bean, coriander, Thai basil, Chinese leaf

Chinese leaves (Peking cabbage)

This delicious crunchy vegetable comes in various sizes, from long, compact barrel-shaped ones to short, squat types. The heads are tightly packed with firm, pale green (or in some cases slightly yellow), crinkled leaves. It is most commonly added to soups and meat stir-fries but its ability to absorb flavours and its pleasant taste and texture make it a favourite with chefs, who like to pair it with rich foods. Store it as you would ordinary cabbage.

Coconut milk

Coconut milk is used extensively in Thailand and elsewhere in Southeast Asia. It has some of the properties of cow's milk – for example, the 'cream' (fatty globules) rises to the top when the milk sits; it must be stirred as it comes to the boil; and its fat is closer in chemical composition to butterfat than to vegetable fat. These qualities make it an important and unusual ingredient in Thai cookery.

The milk itself is the liquid wrung from pressed grated coconut flesh, then combined with water. In Thai cooking it is used in curries and stews and is often combined with curry pastes to make sauces. It is also used as a popular cooling drink and a key ingredient in puddings and sweets.

In Thai markets and, more rarely, Chinese food shops, it may be possible to buy freshly made coconut milk, especially in neighbour-hoods where there is a large Thai or Southeast Asian population. Inexpensive tinned coconut milk can be found readily in supermarkets and Thai food shops. Many brands are high quality and quite acceptable, particularly ones from Thailand and Malaysia. Be sure to shake the tin well before opening.

Coriander (Chinese parsley)

Fresh coriander is one of the most popular herbs used in Thai cooking. It looks like flat-leaf parsley but its pungent, musky, citrus-like flavour gives it a distinctive character that is unmistakable. It is an acquired taste for many people, but one worth the effort.

Its feathery leaves are often used as a garnish, or they can be chopped and mixed into sauces and stuffings. Thai and Chinese grocers stock it, as do many greengrocers and, increasingly, local supermarkets.

When buying fresh coriander, choose deep-green, fresh-looking leaves. Limp, yellowing leaves indicate age and should be avoided. To store coriander, wash it in cold water, dry thoroughly (preferably in a salad spinner) and wrap it in kitchen paper. Put it in the vegetable compartment of your refrigerator, where it should keep for several days.

Coriander, ground

Ground coriander has a fresh, sweet, lemony taste and is widely used in curry mixes. It can be purchased ready ground but, for the best flavour, toast whole coriander seeds in the oven and then grind them yourself.

Curry powder, Madras

Although Western-style curry powders are quite different from those used in Indian cuisine, there are many reliable commercial brands that serve very well. These are used by Thai cooks, because their exotic flavours and subtle aromas add so much to any dish. Remember, curry is a term that refers to a style of cooking and not to a single taste or spice.

Dried shrimp

These are tiny peeled shrimp that have been dried in the sun. A small amount enriches the flavour of an entire dish and they are therefore quite economical. Choose ones that are bright pink-orange in colour. They are sold in small packages in Chinese and Asian supermarkets. Unfortunately there is no substitute for this unique seasoning.

Galangal

This rhizome is related to ginger and is commonly known as Thai or Siamese ginger. Creamy white in colour, with distinctive pink shoots, it has a hot, peppery flavour and is used extensively in Thai cooking – usually mixed with chillies and other spices and herbs to make a base for curries, soups and stews. The Thais believe it has medicinal value, too. If it is unavailable, substitute fresh ginger.

Garlic

This common, nutritious and very popular seasoning is used by Thai cooks in numerous ways – whole, finely chopped, crushed and pickled – to flavour curries, sauces, soups and practically every Thai dish on the menu. Thai garlic has smaller cloves and a milder flavour than Western varieties, with a delicate pink skin that the Thais do not remove before use. In the absence of Thai garlic, select fresh Western garlic that is firm and preferably pinkish in colour. It should be stored in a cool, dry place but not the refrigerator, where it can easily become mildewed or begin sprouting.

Ginger

Fresh root ginger is an indispensable ingredient in Thai cooking, and is even referred to as 'king' in Thailand. Its pungent, spicy taste adds a subtle but distinctive flavour to soups, meats and vegetables and it is also an important seasoning for fish and seafood, since it neutralizes fishy smells.

Root ginger looks rather like a gnarled Jerusalem artichoke and can vary in length from 7.5–15 cm (3–6 in) long. Select firm, unshrivelled pieces and peel off the skin before use. It will keep in the refrigerator, well wrapped in clingfilm, for up to 2 weeks. Dried powdered ginger has a quite different flavour and should be used only as a last resort.

Clockwise from top left: garlic, galangal, ginger and dried shrimp

Kaffir lime leaves

From the kaffir lime tree, this ingredient is a Southeast Asian original. The lime itself is green and about the size of a small orange. Its juice is used in Thai cooking but it is the leaves (*makrut* in Thai) that are highly prized. They have a singular lemon-lime flavour, at the edge of bitter, and add a special dimension to many dishes, including curries, soups and stews. Added to sauces, they slowly release their citrus flavours during cooking. Substitute lime zest if kaffir lime leaves are unavailable.

Lemon grass

This herb is close to being the 'signature' ingredient of Thai cookery. No other cuisine, the Vietnamese excepted, uses it as intensively and extensively. Its subtle, lemony fragrance and flavour impart a very special cachet to delicate dishes, and it is the key ingredient in the famous Thai soup, *tom yam ghoong*, as well as in many other specialities.

As is typical of Thai cuisine, lemon grass is considered a medicinal agent as well as a spice and is often prescribed for digestive disorders. It is closely related to citronella grass. The latter, however, has a stronger oil content and is more likely to be used commercially in perfumes and as a mosquito repellent. The two should not be confused.

Lemon grass is available both fresh and dried. Fresh lemon grass is sold in stalks up to 60 cm (2 feet) long. Most recipes use only the bottom few inches. It is a fibrous plant but this is no problem because what is wanted is its fragrance and taste, and the pieces are always removed after the dish is cooked. Some recipes may call for lemon grass to be finely chopped or pounded into a paste, in which cases it becomes an integral part of the dish.

Try to buy the freshest possible lemon grass, which is usually found in Thai markets or other Asian markets. Avoid dried lemon grass for cooking, as it is mostly used for herbal teas. Fresh lemon grass can be kept, loosely wrapped, in the bottom of the refrigerator for up to one week. Please note that lemon cannot be used as a substitute for the unique flavours of lemon grass.

Lime

This small, green citrus fruit is a native of Southern Asia but has become a global

Clockwise from left: lemon grass stalks, kaffir lime leaves, fresh lime

favourite. It has a delicate, fresh, tart flavour that is widely used to give dishes a 'lift' or as a base for sauces. The refreshing juice and the zest create a unique taste dimension in many Thai dishes. Thai limes are smaller and darker than the ones familiar to us in the West but are just as juicy and aromatic.

Noodles

Only rice is more important than noodles in Thai cuisine. Like rice, they form the basis of nutritious, quick, sustaining meals, as well as light snacks. Several styles of Thai noodle dishes have made their way to the West, including ones made with fresh thin egg noodles, thicker egg or wheat noodles and the popular thin and thick rice noodles. Both fresh and dried kinds are available in Thai and Chinese markets.

Bean thread (transparent) noodles

Also called cellophane noodles, these very fine white noodles are made from ground mung beans. They are available dried, packed in neat, plastic-wrapped bundles, from Thai and Chinese markets and supermarkets. Bean thread noodles are never served on their own but are added to soups or braises, or deep-fried and used as a garnish. Soak them in warm water for about 5 minutes before use. As they are rather long, you might find it easier to cut them into shorter lengths after soaking. If you are frying them, they do not need soaking beforehand but they do need to be separated. The best way to do this is to pull them apart in a large paper bag, which prevents them flying all over the place.

Rice noodles

These dried noodles are opaque white and come in a variety of shapes and thicknesses. One of the most common is rice stick noodles, which are flat and about the length of a chopstick. Rice noodles are very easy to prepare. Simply soak them in warm water for 25 minutes until they are soft, then drain in a colander or sieve. They are now ready to be used in soups or stir-fries.

Wheat noodles and egg noodles

Available dried or fresh, these are made from hard or soft wheat flour and water and sometimes egg, in which case they are labelled as egg noodles. Flat noodles are usually used in soups, while rounded ones are best for frying. The fresh ones freeze well if they are lightly wrapped. Thaw thoroughly before cooking.

Dried wheat or fresh egg noodles are very good blanched and served as an accompaniment to main dishes instead of plain rice. Cook them in boiling water for 3–5 minutes, then drain and serve. If you are cooking noodles ahead of time or before stir-frying them, toss the cooked drained noodles in 2 teaspoons of sesame oil and put them into a bowl. Cover with clingfilm and refrigerate for up to 2 hours.

Oils

Oil is the most common cooking medium in Thailand, although animal fats, usually lard and chicken fat, are used in some areas. Thai cooks tend to use simple vegetable oil made from rapeseed but my favourite is groundnut oil.

To re-use oil after deep-frying, let it cool, then filter it through muslin or a fine sieve into a jar. Cover it tightly and store in a cool, dry place. If you keep it in the refrigerator it will become cloudy, but it will clarify again when it returns to room temperature. I find oils are best re-used just once, since their saturated fat content increases the more you use them.

Groundnut oil

This is also known as peanut or arachide oil. I like to use it for Thai cooking because it has a pleasant, unobtrusive taste. Although it has a higher saturated fat content than some oils, its ability to be heated to a high temperature without burning makes it perfect for stir-frying and deep-frying. Most supermarkets stock groundnut oil but if you cannot find it, use corn oil instead.

Corn oil

Corn or maize oil is also quite suitable for Thai cooking, since it has a high heating point. However, I find it rather bland and with a slightly disagreeable smell. It is high in polyunsaturates and is therefore one of the healthier oils.

Other vegetable oils

Some of the cheaper vegetable oils available include soya, safflower and sunflower. Light in colour and taste, these can also be used in Thai cooking, but take care, since they smoke and burn at lower temperatures than groundnut oil.

Sesame oil
This thick, rich, golden brown oil made from sesame seeds has a distinctive, nutty flavour and aroma. It is widely used in Thai cookery as a seasoning but is not normally used as a cooking oil because it burns easily. Think of it more as a flavouring. A small amount is often added at the last moment to finish a dish.

Peppercorns

Black peppercorns
Black peppercorns are unripe berries from a vine, *Piper nigrum*, which are picked, fermented and then left to dry until they are hard and black. They are best when freshly ground. Until chillies were introduced to Thailand in the sixteenth century, black pepper provided the 'heat' in Thai cooking. Even now, it is an essential ingredient in marinades, pastes and condiments.

White peppercorns
White peppercorns are made from the largest ripe berries, which are suspended in running water for several days until they swell up, so that the skin can be removed more easily. The pale seeds are sun-dried, which turns them a light beige colour – hence, white peppercorns.

Prawns
For the recipes in this book you will need large raw prawns, usually sold as Pacific or king prawns. Most Thai and Chinese food shops, many fishmongers and some supermarkets stock them frozen and in the shell, and they are quite reasonably priced. Fresh prawns are also available but these tend to have been cooked, and in many cases over-cooked. Frozen raw prawns are preferable, as the ready-cooked ones will not absorb the flavours of the sauce you cook them in.

To shell prawns, twist off and discard the head, then open up the shell along the belly and peel it off, together with the tiny legs (the tail shell can be left on for presentation, if liked). Large prawns should also be de-veined by making a shallow cut down the back of each prawn and pulling out the dark intestinal vein that runs along it. Wash the prawns before use. A Chinese trick for improving raw frozen

Clockwise from top left: egg noodles, vermicelli rice noodles, rice stick noodles and bean thread noodles

prawns after shelling and de-veining is to rinse them 3 times in 1 tablespoon of salt and 1.2 litres (2 pints) cold water, changing the salt and water each time. This helps to firm the texture of the prawns and gives them a crystalline, clean taste.

Rice, Thai jasmine
This fragrant long-grain rice is prized for its nutty, aromatic flavour and is much favoured by Thai cooks. There is a certain inscrutability at work here: I have read that, 'The taste of jasmine is not quite perceptible, but you sense that the rice is pleasingly different.' And there *is* a difference, however subtle.

Steamed rice
Steaming is a simple, direct and efficient cooking method for rice. For Thai cooking, I prefer to use jasmine rice, Indian basmati or any other superior long-grain white rice, which

Above: Thai jasmine rice, wonton skins and rice paper underneath

will be dry and fluffy when cooked. Avoid pre-cooked or 'easy-cook' rice, as it lacks the full flavour and the texture of good long-grain rice.

The secret of preparing rice without it becoming sticky is to cook it first in an uncovered pot at a high heat until most of the water has evaporated. Then the heat should be turned very low, the pan covered, and the rice cooked slowly in the remaining steam. Never uncover the pan once the steaming process has begun; just time it and wait.

Here is a good trick to remember: if you cover the rice with about 2.5 cm (1 in) of water it should always cook properly without sticking. Many packet recipes for rice use too much water, resulting in a gluey mess. Follow my method and you will have perfect steamed rice.

For 4 people you will need enough long-grain rice to fill a measuring jug to 400 ml (14 fl oz). Put the rice in a large bowl and wash it in several changes of water until the water becomes clear. Drain the rice, put it into a heavy pan with 600 ml (1 pint) water and bring to the boil. Boil for about 5 minutes, until most of the surface liquid has evaporated. The surface of the rice should have small indentations like a pitted crater. At this point, cover the pan with a very tight-fitting lid, turn the heat as low as possible and let the rice cook undisturbed for 15 minutes. There is no need to 'fluff' the rice; just let it rest off the heat for 5 minutes before serving.

Rice paper

Rice paper is made from a mixture of rice flour, water and salt, which is rolled out by machine until paper-thin, then dried on bamboo mats in the sun, giving the translucent sheets their beautiful cross-hatch imprint. Although more identified with Vietnamese cooking, it is also used by Thai cooks for wrapping spring rolls. I prefer to use rice paper for this, as it absorbs less oil then wheat-based wrappers.

Rice paper is available from Thai and Chinese food shops and some supermarkets, in packets of 50–100 round or triangular sheets. All brands are good, especially the ones from Vietnam and Thailand. Choose white-looking rice paper and avoid yellowish ones, which may be too old. Broken pieces in the pack can also indicate age.

Store rice paper in a cool, dry place. After use, wrap the remaining rice papers carefully in the pack they came in, put this in another plastic bag and seal well before storing.

Sauces and pastes

Thai cookery involves a number of tasty sauces and pastes, some light, some thick. They are essential for authentic Thai cooking and it is well worth making the effort to obtain them. Most are sold in bottles or tins by Thai and Chinese food shops and some supermarkets. Once opened, tinned sauces should be transferred to screw-top glass jars and kept in the refrigerator, where they will last indefinitely.

Chilli bean sauce

This thick, dark sauce or paste is made from soya beans, chillies and other seasonings, and is very hot and spicy. Be sure to seal the jar tightly after use and store it in the larder or refrigerator. Do not confuse it with chilli sauce, which is a hotter, redder, thinner sauce made without beans and used mainly as a dipping sauce for cooked dishes.

Fish sauce

Fish sauce, or *nam pla*, is also known as fish gravy and is a Thai standard. It is a thin brown liquid made from fermented salted fish, usually anchovies, and has a noticeably fishy odour and salty taste. If you are not used to it, add it sparingly at first. Bear in mind, though, that cooking greatly diminishes the fishy flavour, and the sauce does add a special richness and quality to dishes. The Thai brands are especially good, with a less salty taste. Fish sauce is an inexpensive ingredient, so buy the best on offer.

Oyster sauce

This thick, brown sauce is made from a concentrate of oysters cooked in soy sauce and brine. Despite its name, it does not taste fishy. It has a rich flavour and is used not only in cooking but also as a condiment, diluted with a little oil, for vegetables, poultry and meat. It is usually sold in bottles and can be bought in Chinese and Thai food shops and supermarkets. I find it keeps best in the refrigerator. A vegetarian oyster sauce made with mushrooms is now available.

Shrimp paste/shrimp sauce

This is made from pulverized salted shrimp

that is left to ferment. For shrimp paste, the mixture is dried in the sun and cut into cakes. Shrimp sauce, however, is packed directly into jars while thick and moist. Once packed, the light pink sauce slowly turns a greyish shade, acquiring a pungent flavour as it matures. Popular in Thai cooking, it adds a distinctive flavour and fragrance to dishes – similar to anchovy paste, but stronger.

Although the odour of shrimp sauce is assertive, remember that the cooking process quickly tames its aroma and taste. Available in Thai and Chinese food shops, the best brands of shrimp sauce are from Thailand. It will last indefinitely if stored in the refrigerator.

Soy sauce

Soy sauce is an essential ingredient in Thai cooking. It is made from a mixture of soya beans, flour and water, which is then fermented naturally and aged for some months. The liquid that is finally distilled is soy sauce.

There are two main types. Light soy sauce, as the name implies, is light in colour, but it is full of flavour and is the better one to use for cooking. It is saltier than dark soy sauce, and is known in Chinese and Thai food shops as Superior Soy.

Dark soy sauce, confusingly, is known as Soy Superior Sauce. It is aged for much longer than light soy sauce, hence its darker, almost black colour, and is also slightly thicker and stronger. It is more suitable for stews. I prefer it to light soy as a dipping sauce.

Most soy sauce sold in supermarkets is dark soy. Chinese and Thai food shops sell both types and the quality is excellent. Be sure you buy the correct one, as the names are very similar.

Thai curry paste

This is an intensely flavoured paste of herbs and spices, used in coconut curries, soups and other dishes. Red curry paste is made with dried red chillies and green curry paste with fresh green chillies – remember that the green chillies are much stronger than the red.

Curry paste is time-consuming to prepare, and even in Thailand many cooks buy it at their favourite shop rather than making it themselves. Fortunately, high-quality ready-made curry pastes are available in shops and supermarkets elsewhere, too.

Sesame seeds

These are the dried seeds of the sesame herb. They have a pleasing nutty flavour and are rich in protein and minerals. Unhulled, the seeds range from greyish white to black in colour. The tiny hulled seeds are cream coloured and pointed at one end. Stored in a glass jar in a cool, dry place, they will keep indefinitely.

To toast sesame seeds, heat a frying-pan, then add the seeds and stir occasionally. Watch them closely to make sure they don't burn. When they begin to brown lightly, after about 3–5 minutes, stir them again and tip them on to a plate. Leave to cool, then store in a glass jar in a cool, dark place.

Alternatively, you could spread the sesame seeds on a baking sheet and roast them in an oven preheated to 160°C/325°F/Gas Mark 3 for 10–15 minutes, until lightly browned.

Shallots

These mild-flavoured members of the onion family are very popular in Thailand, where the local version is readily available. They are small – about the size of pickling onions – with copper-red skins, and have a distinctive onion flavour without being as strong as overpowering as ordinary onions. Western-style shallots make an excellent substitute for Thai shallots, which are difficult to find even in some Thai food shops. They are quite expensive but their sweet flavour permeates food, and a few go a long way. Keep them in a cool, dry place (not the refrigerator) and peel, slice or chop them as you would an onion.

Shaoxing rice wine

As a seasoning, wine is not crucial to traditional Thai cookery but it is now being used in Thailand more and more. It has been an important component of Chinese cooking for centuries, and I believe the finest is produced in Shaoxing in Zhejiang Province in eastern China. It is made from glutinous rice, yeast and spring water. Now readily available in Chinese and Thai markets and in some wine shops in the West, it should be kept tightly corked at room temperature. A good-quality, dry pale sherry can be substituted but cannot match its rich, mellow taste. Do not confuse this wine with sake, which is the Japanese version of rice wine and quite different. Western grape wines are not an adequate substitute either.

Clockwise from top left: fish sauce, green curry paste, chilli bean sauce, oyster sauce, shrimp paste and red curry paste

Clockwise from left: madras curry powder, sesame seeds and mung beans

Sugar

Sugar has been used – sparingly – in the cooking of savoury dishes in Thailand for centuries. Properly employed, it helps balance the flavours of sauces and other dishes. Thai palm sugar, which comes in brown slabs or large lumps, is rich and has a more subtle flavour than refined sugar. It also gives a good lustre, or glaze, to braised dishes and sauces. You can buy it in Thai and Chinese food shops, where it is usually sold in packets, although some chefs prefer the canned version. You may need to break the slabs or lumps into smaller pieces with a wooden mallet or rolling pin.

If you cannot find Thai sugar, use white sugar or coffee sugar crystals (the amber, chunky kind) instead. Light brown sugar mixed with an equal part of molasses may also serve as a substitute.

Vinegar

Vinegars are widely used in Thai cooking. Unlike Western vinegars, they are usually made from rice. There are many varieties, ranging in flavour from spicy and slightly tart to sweet and pungent. They can be bought in Thai shops and supermarkets and will keep indefinitely. If you cannot find these vinegars I suggest you use cider vinegar instead. Malt vinegar can be substituted if necessary but its taste is stronger and more acidic. In some dishes Thai chefs have taken to using a good-quality Western-style white vinegar, prized for its sharp tang. But never simply substitute white vinegar for rice vinegar – the contrast is too great.

Chinese white rice vinegar

This clear vinegar has a mild flavour with a faint taste of glutinous rice. It is used in sweet and sour dishes.

Black rice vinegar

Black rice vinegar is very dark in colour and rich, though mild, in taste. It is used for braised dishes, sauces, and sometimes as a dipping sauce for crab.

Red rice vinegar

This is sweet and spicy and is normally used as a dipping sauce for seafood.

Winged beans

These unusual pods are popular in Thailand, prized for their delicate, asparagus-like flavour. They are bright green and the short, square beans have a decorative frill along their sides, from which they get their name. They are often blanched and served in a salad dressed with an aromatic sauce. Runner beans or French beans make a good substitute.

Wonton skins

These thin, yellowish, pastry-like wrappings made from egg and flour can be stuffed with minced meat and then fried, steamed or used in soups. They are available fresh or frozen from Chinese and Thai food shops, sold in small batches of 8 cm (3¼ in) squares, wrapped in plastic. The number of skins in a packet varies from about 30 to 36, depending on the supplier. Fresh wonton skins will keep for about 5 days in the refrigerator if stored in clingfilm or a plastic bag. If you are using frozen wonton skins, just peel off the number you require and thaw them thoroughly.

Wonton skins must not be confused with the much more delicate rice paper wrappers (see page 17).

EQUIPMENT

Special equipment is not essential for Thai cooking. Despite the complexities of ingredients, colours, tastes and textures, preparing Thai food is simple and straightforward. However, there are a few tools, tested over many centuries of use, that make the task much easier. Once you become familiar with woks, for example, you will have entered the culinary world of Thailand and, indeed, all of Southeast Asia. As a bonus you will find that such tools are also helpful in preparing your own favourite dishes.

Wok

Like the Chinese, the Thais use the wok in preparing almost every meal. The most versatile piece of cooking equipment ever invented, it may be used for stir-frying, blanching, deep-frying and steaming. Its shape permits fuel-efficient, quick and even cooking. When stir-frying, the deep sides prevent the food spilling over; when deep-frying, much less oil is required because of the wok's tapered base.

There are two basic types: the traditional Cantonese version, with short, rounded handles on either side, and the *pau*, sometimes called the Peking wok, which has one 30–35 cm (12–14 in) long handle. The long-handled wok keeps you at a safer distance from the possibility of splashing hot oil or water.

The standard round-bottomed wok may only be used on gas hobs. Ones with flatter bottoms are now available, designed especially for electric hobs. Although this shape really defeats the purpose of the traditional design, which is to concentrate intense heat at the centre, it does have the advantage over ordinary frying-pans because it has deeper sides.

Choosing a wok

Choose a large wok – preferably about 30–35 cm (12–14 in) in diameter, with deep sides. It is easier – and safer – to cook a small batch of food in a large wok than a large quantity in a small one. Be aware that some modernized woks are too shallow or too flat-bottomed and thus no better than a frying-pan. A heavier wok, preferably made of carbon steel, is superior to the lighter stainless steel or aluminium type, which cannot take very high heat and tends to blacken, as well as scorch the food. Good non-stick carbon steel woks that maintain the heat without sticking are now available. They need special care to prevent scratching but in recent years the non-stick technology has improved vastly, so that they can now be safely recommended. They are especially useful when cooking food that has a high acid content, such as lemons.

Thai woks are generally made of brass and have a wider, flatter base, but they essentially do the same job as the Chinese wok.

Seasoning a wok

All woks except non-stick ones should be seasoned before first use. Many need to be scrubbed as well, to remove the machine oil that is applied to the surface by the manufacturer to protect it in transit. This is the only time you will ever need to scrub your wok – unless you let it become rusty.

Scrub it with a cream cleanser and water to remove as much of the machine oil as possible. Then dry it and put it on the hob on a low heat. Add 2 tablespoons of cooking oil and, using a wad of kitchen paper, rub the oil over the inside of the wok until the entire surface is lightly coated. Heat the wok slowly for about 10–15 minutes and then wipe it thoroughly with more kitchen paper. The paper will become blackened from the machine oil. Repeat this process of coating, heating and wiping until the kitchen paper comes away clean. Your wok will darken and become well seasoned with use, which is a good sign.

Cleaning a wok

Once your wok has been seasoned, you should never scrub it with soap or water. Just wash it in plain clean water and dry it thoroughly after each use – putting the cleaned wok over a low heat for a minute or two should do the trick. If it does rust a bit, scrub it with a cream cleanser and re-season it. With ordinary usage and care, the versatile wok will serve you faithfully through countless meals.

Stir-frying in a wok

The most important thing when stir-frying is to have all your ingredients ready and to hand –

Above: wok with lid, spatula, chopsticks, cleaver and rack

this is a very fast method of cooking and you will not have time to stop and chop things while you are cooking.

Heat the wok until it is very hot, then add the oil and distribute it evenly over the surface using a metal spatula or long-handled spoon. It should be very hot – almost smoking – before you add the ingredients.

Add the food to be cooked and stir-fry by tossing it around the wok or pan with a metal spatula or long-handled spoon. If you are stir-frying meat, let each side rest for a few seconds before continuing to stir. Keep moving the food from the centre of the wok to the sides.

I prefer to use a long-handled wok, as there can be a lot of splattering due to the high temperature at which the food must be cooked.

Wok accessories

Wok stand
This is a metal ring or frame designed to keep a conventionally shaped wok steady on the hob. It is essential if you want to use your wok for steaming, deep-frying or braising. Stands come in two designs: a solid metal ring punched with about six ventilation holes, and a thin, circular wire frame. If you have a gas cooker use only the latter type, as the more solid design does not allow for sufficient ventilation and may lead to a build-up of gas, which could put the flame out completely.

Wok lid
This light, inexpensive domed cover, usually made from aluminium, is used for steaming. It is normally supplied with the wok but if not, may be purchased at a Chinese or Asian market, or you may use any domed saucepan lid that fits snugly.

Spatula
A long-handled metal spatula shaped rather like a small shovel is ideal for scooping and tossing food in a wok. Alternatively any good long-handled spoon can be used. Thai spatulas are commonly made of coconut shells.

Rack
When steaming food in your wok, you will need a wooden or metal rack or trivet to raise the food above the water level. Wok sets usually include a rack but, if not, Asian and Chinese shops sell them separately. Department stores and hardware shops also sell wooden and metal stands, which can serve the same purpose. Any rack, improvised or not, that keeps the food above the water so that it is steamed and not boiled will suffice.

Bamboo brush
This bundle of stiff, split bamboo is used for cleaning a wok without scrubbing away the seasoned surface. It is an attractive, inexpensive implement but not essential. A soft washing-up brush will do just as well.

Chopping board
One decided improvement over traditional Thai cooking implements is the modern chopping board made of hardwood or white acrylic. Typical Thai chopping boards are made of soft wood, which is difficult to maintain and, being soft, provides a fertile surface for bacteria. Hardwood or white acrylic boards are easy to clean, resist bacterial accumulation, and last much longer.

Thai cooking entails much chopping, slicing and dicing, so it is essential to have a large, steady chopping board. For reasons of hygiene, never place cooked meat on a board on which raw meat or poultry has been prepared. For raw meat, always use a separate board and clean it thoroughly after each use.

Chopsticks
It may come as a surprise to discover that Thais do not normally eat with chopsticks. Although many Thai restaurants in the West place chopsticks at their diners' disposal, in Thailand they are normally found only in Chinese restaurants. Thais eat with knives and forks. However, you may enjoy serving Thai food with chopsticks. Many Western diners find them a challenge but I always encourage their use. Attempting any new technique is an interesting experience, and chopsticks do indeed offer the novice a physical *entrée* into many Asian cuisines – a hands-on experience, if you will. Chopsticks can also be used for stirring, beating, whipping and mixing. But of course you can get along nicely with Western spoons, forks, ladles, spatulas and whisks.

Chopsticks are cheap and readily available. I prefer the wooden ones but in China plastic ones are more commonly used (and re-used) for hygienic and economic reasons.

Clockwise from top: rice cooker, pestle and mortar for grinding spices, bamboo steamer

Cleaver

To Thai cooks, as to Chinese, the cleaver is an all-purpose cutting instrument that makes all other knives redundant. Once you acquire some skill with a cleaver, you will see how it can be used on all types of food to slice, dice, chop, fillet, shred, crush or whatever. Most Asian chefs rely upon three different sizes of cleaver – light, medium and heavy – to be used as appropriate. Of course, you may use your own familiar kitchen knives instead, but if you decide to invest in a cleaver, choose a good-quality stainless steel model and keep it well sharpened.

Deep-fat fryer

A deep-fat fryer is very useful and you may find it safer and easier to use for deep-frying than a wok. The quantities of oil given in the recipes in this book are based on the amount required for deep-frying in a wok. If you are using a deep-fat fryer instead, you will need about double that amount, but never fill it more than half-full with oil.

Rice cooker

Electric rice cookers are increasing in popularity. They cook rice perfectly and keep it warm throughout the meal. They also have the advantage of freeing a burner or element so the hob is less cluttered. They are relatively expensive, however, so are only worth buying if you eat rice frequently.

Steamer

Steaming is not a very popular cooking method in the West. This is unfortunate because it is the best way of preparing many foods with a delicate taste and texture, such as fish and vegetables. In Thailand, bamboo steamers have been in use for many centuries. They come in several sizes, of which the 25-cm (10-in) one is the most suitable for home use. The food is placed in the steamer, which is then placed above boiling water in a wok or pot. To stop the food sticking to the steamer as it cooks, put it on a layer of clean, damp muslin. A tight-fitting bamboo lid prevents the steam escaping; several steamers, stacked one above the other, may be used simultaneously.

Before using a bamboo steamer for the first time, wash it and then steam it empty for about 5 minutes. Of course, any kind of wide metal steamer may be used if you prefer.

Miscellaneous

Stainless steel bowls of different sizes, along with sieves and colanders, complete the list of basic implements. They are very useful because you will often have to drain or strain oils and juices and because you will be doing much mixing of wonderful foods. It is better to have one too many tools than one too few.

Conversion tables

Conversions are approximate and have been rounded up or down. Follow one set of measurements only – do not mix metric and Imperial.

Weights		Volume		Measurements	
Metric	**Imperial**	**Metric**	**Imperial**	**Metric**	**Imperial**
15 g	½ oz	25 ml	1 fl oz	0.5 cm	¼ inch
25 g	1 oz	50 ml	2 fl oz	1 cm	½ inch
40 g	1½ oz	85 ml	3 fl oz	2.5 cm	1 inch
50 g	2 oz	150 ml	5 fl oz (¼ pint)	5 cm	2 inches
75 g	3 oz	300 ml	10 fl oz (½ pint)	7.5 cm	3 inches
100 g	4 oz	450 ml	15 fl oz (¾ pint)	10 cm	4 inches
150 g	5 oz	600 ml	1 pint	15 cm	6 inches
175 g	6 oz	700 ml	1¼ pints	18 cm	7 inches
200 g	7 oz	900 ml	1½ pints	20 cm	8 inches
225 g	8 oz	1 litres	1¾ pints	23 cm	9 inches
250 g	9 oz	1.2 litres	2 pints	25 cm	10 inches
275 g	10 oz	1.25 litres	2¼ pints	30 cm	12 inches
350 g	12 oz	1.5 litres	2½ pints		
375 g	13 oz	1.6 litres	2¾ pints		

Weights		Volume		Oven temperatures		
400 g	14 oz	1.75 litres	3 pints	140°C	275°F	Gas Mk 1
425 g	15 oz	1.8 litres	3¼ pints	150°C	300°F	Gas Mk 2
450 g	1 lb	2 litres	3½ pints	160°C	325°F	Gas Mk 3
550 g	1¼ lb	2.1 litres	3¾ pints	180°C	350°F	Gas Mk 4
675 g	1½ lb	2.25 litres	4 pints	190°C	375°F	Gas Mk 5
900 g	2 lb	2.75 litres	5 pints	200°C	400°F	Gas Mk 6
1.5 kg	3 lb	3.4 litres	6 pints	220°C	425°F	Gas Mk 7
1.75 kg	4 lb	3.9 litres	7 pints	230°C	450°F	Gas Mk 8
2.25 kg	5 lb	5 litres	8 pints (1 gal)	240°C	475°F	Gas Mk 9

SOUPS, SNACKS and STARTERS

Spicy prawn and lemon grass soup

This delicious soup, called *tom yam ghoong*, is one of the most popular with Western fans of Thai food, combining spicy and sour in an enticing mixture of herbs and seasonings. It is not difficult to make and is a fine starting point for any meal.

serves 4
preparation time: 15 minutes, plus 10 minutes' standing
cooking time: 15 minutes

2 fresh lemon grass stalks

1.2 litres (2 pints) home-made fish or chicken stock or good-quality bought stock

8 kaffir lime leaves, cut in half, or 1 tablespoon shredded lime zest

3 fresh red Thai chillies, seeded and finely shredded

¼ teaspoon black pepper

3 tablespoons fish sauce (*nam pla*)

3 tablespoons lime juice

225 g (8 oz) raw prawns, shelled and de-veined (see page 15)

2 spring onions (white and green parts), finely shredded

5 fresh coriander sprigs

1 Peel off the tough outer layers of the lemon grass stalks, leaving the tender whitish centre. Cut it into 7.5 cm (3 in) pieces and crush with the flat of a heavy knife.

2 Bring the stock to a simmer in a large saucepan and add the lemon grass. Reduce the heat, then cover and simmer for 10 minutes. Remove the lemon grass with a slotted spoon and discard.

3 Add the lime leaves or zest, chillies, black pepper, fish sauce and lime juice and simmer for 3 minutes. Now add the prawns, cover the pan and remove from the heat. Leave to stand for 10 minutes.

4 Finally, stir in the spring onions and coriander sprigs. Ladle into a large soup tureen or individual bowls and serve immediately.

Savoury rice soup

This is the Thai version of a gentle rice soup that can be found throughout Asia. The Chinese make it thick and creamy whereas *kao tom*, as it is known in Thailand, is more of a thin broth. However it is made, it is true comfort food, savoury and nurturing. Feel free to add your favourite cooked meat, poultry or seafood, or just serve it simply, with garnishes such as the ones listed below.

serves 2–4
preparation time: 15 minutes
cooking time: 10 minutes

100 g (4 oz) cooked long-grain white rice

1.2 litres (2 pints) home-made chicken stock or good-quality bought stock

3 tablespoons fish sauce (*nam pla*)

Freshly ground black pepper to taste

1½ tablespoons vegetable oil

3 tablespoons finely chopped garlic

For the garnish:

2 spring onions, finely shredded

1 tablespoon finely shredded fresh ginger

1–2 small fresh red or green Thai chillies, seeded and finely shredded

a handful of fresh coriander leaves

1 Combine the cooked rice and stock in a large pan and bring to a simmer. Add the fish sauce and black pepper and simmer for 5 minutes.

2 Heat a wok or large frying-pan over a medium heat until it is hot but not smoking. Add the oil and, when it is hot, stir in the garlic. Lower the heat and stir-fry gently for 20 seconds, until the garlic is lightly browned. Remove and drain on kitchen paper.

3 Pour the rice and stock into the wok and simmer for 2 minutes. Turn into a soup tureen and garnish with the cooked garlic, spring onions, ginger, chillies and coriander leaves. Serve at once.

Northern Thai chicken noodle soup

Khao soi is a wonderfully hearty but distinctly Thai soup, and quite delicious. A perfect dish for a large hungry crowd.

serves 4–6
preparation time: 10 minutes
cooking time: 25 minutes

175 g (6 oz) fresh or dried egg noodles

2 fresh lemon grass stalks

175 g (6 oz) boneless, skinless chicken breasts

1 tablespoon vegetable oil

1 small onion, finely chopped

2 tablespoons coarsely chopped garlic

1.2 litres (2 pints) home made chicken or vegetable stock or good-quality bought stock

1 x 400 ml (14 fl oz) tin of coconut milk

2 small, fresh red or green Thai chillies, seeded and finely shredded

1 tablespoon fish sauce (*nam pla*)

1 tablespoon dark soy sauce

1 tablespoon sugar

2 tablespoons Madras curry paste or powder

1 teaspoon salt

½ teaspoon freshly ground black pepper

2 tablespoons lime juice

a handful of fresh coriander and basil leaves

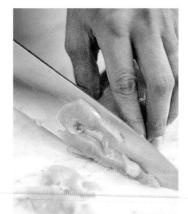

1 Cook the noodles in a large pan of boiling water for 3–5 minutes, until tender. Drain thoroughly and set aside.

2 Peel off the tough outer layers of the lemon grass stalks, leaving the tender whitish centre. Cut it into 7.5 cm (3 in) pieces and crush with the flat of a heavy knife. Shred the chicken into strips.

3 Heat a large, heavy pan over a high heat and add the oil. When it is very hot and slightly smoking, add the onion, garlic and lemon grass and stir-fry for about 3 min- utes. Stir in the stock and coconut milk, turn the heat to low, then cover and simmer for 10 minutes.

4 Add the chillies, chicken, fish sauce, soy sauce, sugar, curry paste or powder, salt and pepper and stir well. Add the drained noodles, then cover and simmer for 5 minutes.

5 Remove the lemon grass with a slotted spoon. Stir in the lime juice, then pour the soup into a large tureen, garnish with the coriander and basil leaves and serve at once.

Coconut chicken soup

No mistaking the Thai heritage here: coconut is a marker of authentic Thai cuisine. This soup, called *tom kha gai*, has a richness one associates with cream but in fact it is due to the coconut milk, whose opulence and aroma add so much to the dish, making it almost a meal in itself.

This recipe is often modified for Western palates by using chicken breasts instead of thighs, but I find that chicken thighs, with their more robust flavour and texture, give the soup a depth and substance that are much more in keeping with the Thai tradition.

serves 4
preparation time: 10 minutes
cooking time: 1¼ hours

2 fresh lemon grass stalks

1.5 litres (2½ pints) home-made chicken stock or good-quality bought stock

2 tablespoons coarsely chopped fresh galangal or ginger

6 kaffir lime leaves or 2 tablespoons coarsely chopped lime zest

6 tablespoons finely sliced shallots

225 g (8 oz) skinless, boneless chicken thighs

3 tablespoons fish sauce (*nam pla*)

4 tablespoons lime juice

2 fresh red or green Thai chillies, seeded and finely shredded

1 tablespoon sugar

1 x 400 ml (14 fl oz) tin of coconut milk

a handful of fresh Thai basil leaves or ordinary basil leaves

1 Peel off the tough outer layers of the lemon grass stalks, leaving the tender whitish centre. Cut it into 7.5 cm (3 in) pieces and crush with the flat of a heavy knife.

2 Put the stock in a large pan with the lemon grass, galangal or ginger, lime leaves or zest and half the shallots. Bring to the boil, then reduce the heat, cover and simmer gently for 1 hour. Strain through a sieve, discarding the lemon grass, galangal, lime and shallots, then return the stock to the pan.

3 Cut the chicken into 2.5 cm (1 in) chunks and add to the strained stock, together with the fish sauce, lime juice, chillies, sugar, coconut milk and the remaining shallots.

4 Bring to the boil, then reduce the heat and simmer for 8 minutes. Transfer the soup to a large tureen, garnish with the basil leaves and serve at once.

Thai-style spring rolls

Although the Chinese influence is evident in this recipe, there is a distinct Thai flavour in each bite – a pungent note not found in traditional Chinese spring rolls. They make a tasty starter for a Thai meal – or any meal, for that matter. In Thailand they are called *poh piah tod*.

makes about 30
preparation time: 30 minutes
cooking time: 25 minutes

5 tablespoons plain flour

1 packet of small, round rice paper wrappers

15 fl oz (450 ml) vegetable oil, for deep-frying

For the spicy dipping sauce:

2–3 small, fresh red Thai chillies, finely chopped (seeded first if you prefer a milder flavour)

1 tablespoon sugar

3 tablespoons fish sauce (*nam pla*) or light soy sauce

3 tablespoons lime juice

2 teaspoons water

For the filling:

1½ tablespoons vegetable oil

3 tablespoons coarsely chopped garlic

175 g (6 oz) fresh crab meat

100 g (4 oz) minced pork

100 g (4 oz) shelled raw prawns, minced or finely chopped

2 tablespoons fish sauce (*nam pla*)

1 tablespoon light soy sauce

1 teaspoon sugar

½ teaspoon freshly ground black pepper

3 tablespoons finely chopped fresh coriander

1 In a small bowl, combine all the ingredients for the spicy dipping sauce. Set aside until ready to serve.

2 Next make the filling for the spring rolls. Heat a wok or large frying-pan over a high heat and add the oil. When it is very hot and slightly smoking, add the garlic and stir-fry for 30 seconds.

3 Add the crab, pork, prawns, fish sauce, soy sauce, sugar and black pepper and stir-fry for 2 minutes. Remove from the heat and stir in the fresh coriander. Leave to cool completely.

4 Put the flour in a small bowl, add 6 tablespoons of water and mix to a paste. Set aside.

5 Fill a large bowl with warm water. Dip one of the rice paper rounds in the water and let it soften, then remove and drain on a tea-towel.

6 Put about a tablespoon of the filling on the softened rice paper wrapper. Fold in each side, roll up tightly and seal the ends with a little of the flour paste. You should have a roll about 5 cm (2 in) long, rather like a small sausage. Repeat with the remaining wrappers and filling. You may need to change the water occasionally as it cools.

7 Heat the oil in a deep-fat fryer or large wok and deep-fry the spring rolls, a few at a time, for about 3 minutes, until golden brown and crisp. (Do not fry too many at once, as they have a tendency to stick together. If this happens, simply break them apart after they are cooked.) Drain on kitchen paper and serve at once with the dipping sauce.

Spicy papaya salad

In hot and humid Thailand, room-temperature salads such as this *som tam* often accompany meals. Their spicy coolness makes them the perfect balance for heavier dishes and the bonus is that they can be prepared ahead of time. Green papaya works best here because it is slightly tart, with the crispness of a fresh apple. You will find the crunchy texture and spicy flavours of this salad quite addictive. Serve as a starter or an accompaniment.

serves 4
preparation time: 15 minutes

1 green, unripe papaya

2 small, fresh red Thai chillies, seeded and chopped

2 garlic cloves, crushed

2 tablespoons chopped shallots

½ teaspoon salt

2 tablespoons lime juice

1 tablespoon fish sauce (*nam pla*)

1 tablespoon sugar

To garnish:

3–4 tablespoons crushed roasted peanuts

2 small, fresh red Thai chillies, seeded and sliced (optional)

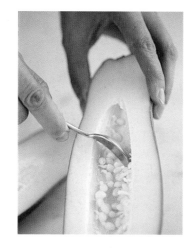

1 Peel the papaya and cut it in half lengthways. Remove the seeds and finely shred the flesh.

2 Put the chillies, garlic, shallots and salt in a mortar and pestle. Add a quarter of the shredded papaya and pound gently until it is slightly softened (if you don't have a mortar and pestle, simply stir the ingredients together or crush them against the side of a bowl with a wooden spoon). Continue to add more of the shredded papaya until it is completely used up.

3 Add the lime juice, fish sauce and sugar. Toss carefully and arrange on a platter. Garnish with the crushed peanuts and the sliced chillies, if using.

Crispy wontons with sweet chilli sauce

Savoury crispy wontons are familiar to lovers of Chinese food but the Thai version, *kiew grob thai*, is just as popular. These delectable treats can be prepared ahead of time and frozen before deep-frying. They make an ideal starter for a Thai-style meal or they can simply be served with drinks.

Although there are many commercial chilli sauces available, nothing beats the taste of a freshly made sauce such as this one. It can be kept in the fridge for up to a week.

serves 6
preparation time: 45 minutes
cooking time: 30 minutes

225 g (8 oz) wonton skins, thawed if necessary

600 ml (1 pint) vegetable oil, for deep-frying

For the sweet chilli sauce:

175 g (6 oz) large, fresh red chillies, finely chopped (seeded first if you prefer a milder flavour)

3 tablespoons coarsely chopped garlic

1 tablespoon sugar

1 tablespoon white rice vinegar or malt vinegar

1 tablespoon fish sauce (*nam pla*)

1 tablespoon vegetable oil

salt to taste

150 ml (5 fl oz) water

For the filling:

100 g (4 oz) raw prawns, shelled, de-veined (see page 15) and coarsely chopped

350 g (12 oz) minced fatty pork

2 teaspoons salt

1 teaspoon freshly ground black pepper

2 tablespoons finely chopped garlic

3 tablespoons finely chopped spring onions

2 tablespoons fish sauce (*nam pla*)

1 teaspoon sugar

3 tablespoons finely chopped fresh coriander

1 egg, lightly beaten

1 Put all the ingredients for the sweet chilli sauce in a wok or saucepan and bring to the boil. Turn the heat very low, cover and simmer gently for 15 minutes. Remove from the heat and leave to cool.

2 Purée the mixture in a blender or food processor until it is a smooth paste. Reheat in a wok or saucepan for about 3 minutes to bring out the flavour, adding more salt if necessary. Once cool, it is ready to use or can be stored in the refrigerator.

3 Next make the filling for the wontons. Put the prawns and pork in a large bowl, add the salt and pepper and mix well, either by kneading with your hand or by stirring with a wooden spoon.

4 Add the rest of the filling ingredients and stir them well into the prawn and pork mixture. Cover with clingfilm and chill for at least 20 minutes.

6 Heat a wok or large frying-pan over a high heat and add the oil. When it is hot, add a handful of wontons and deep-fry for 3 minutes, until golden and crisp. (If the oil gets too hot, reduce the heat slightly.) Drain well on kitchen paper and then fry the remaining wontons. Serve immediately, with the sweet chilli sauce.

5 To stuff the wontons, put about a tablespoon of the filling in the centre of each wonton skin. Dampen the edges with a little water and bring them up around the filling. Pinch the edges together at the top so that the wonton is sealed; it should look like a small filled bag.

Tasty fried prawns

This Thai dish, *ghoong thod*, is characteristically elegant and complex in taste. The secret is the marination of the prawns. They are then surprisingly simple to cook, as they are deep-fried very quickly.

serves 4
preparation time: 30 minutes,
  plus 2 hours' marinating
cooking time: 15 minutes

450 g (1 lb) raw prawns, shelled and de-veined (see page 15)

plain flour, for dusting

600 ml (1 pint) vegetable oil, for deep-frying

For the marinade:

3 dried red chillies, chopped

2 tablespoons chopped shallots

3 tablespoons coarsely chopped garlic

2 tablespoons finely chopped fresh galangal or ginger

3 tablespoons chopped coriander root or coriander stalks

1 tablespoon fish sauce (*nam pla*)

1 tablespoon lime juice

50 ml (2 fl oz) tinned coconut milk

2 teaspoons water

1 Briefly process all the marinade ingredients together in a blender or food processor. Pour the marinade over the prawns and mix well. Chill for at least 2 hours.

2 Drain the marinade from the prawns, scraping off any bits; discard the marinade. Dust the prawns with flour, shaking off any excess.

3 Heat a wok or large frying-pan over a high heat and add the oil. When it is very hot and slightly smoking, add a handful of prawns and deep-fry for 3 minutes, until golden and crisp. If the oil gets too hot, reduce the heat slightly. Drain the prawns well on kitchen paper and fry the remaining prawns. Serve immediately.

Crispy corn cakes

These make a wonderfully enticing starter – a savoury mixture of corn and pork fried to crispy morsels. To expedite matters when you are cooking for a dinner party, you could partially fry the corn cakes beforehand and then plunge them into hot oil again just before serving. Serve them with Sweet chilli sauce (see page 42). Their Thai name is *tod mun khao phod*.

serves 4–6
preparation time: 15 minutes
cooking time: 15 minutes

450 g (1 lb) corn on the cob,
   or 275 g (10 oz) tinned
   sweetcorn

175 g (6 oz) minced fatty pork

2 tablespoons finely chopped
   fresh coriander

2 tablespoons finely chopped
   garlic

2 tablespoons fish sauce
   (*nam pla*)

½ teaspoon freshly ground
   white pepper

1 teaspoon sugar

1 tablespoon cornflour

2 eggs, beaten

600 ml (1 pint) vegetable oil,
   for deep-frying

To garnish:

a handful of fresh coriander
   sprigs

1 small cucumber, peeled and
   thinly sliced

1 If using corn on the cob, strip off the husks and the silk and cut off the kernels with a sharp knife or cleaver. You should end up with about 275 g (10 oz). If you are using tinned corn, drain it well.

2 Put half the corn in a blender, add all the remaining ingredients except the oil and blend to a purée. Pour this mixture into a bowl and stir in the rest of the corn.

3 Heat a wok or large frying-pan over a high heat and add the oil. When it is very hot and slightly smoking, pour in a small ladleful of the corn mixture. Repeat until the wok is full. Reduce the heat to low and cook for 1–2 minutes, until the fritters are brown underneath, then turn them over and fry the other side.

4 Remove the fritters from the wok with a slotted spoon and drain on kitchen paper. Keep them warm while you cook the remaining fritters. Arrange on a warm platter, garnish with the coriander and sliced cucumber and serve at once.

Spicy pomelo salad

The pomelo is similar to a grapefruit but larger, seedless and with a thicker skin. It is very popular in Thailand, particularly in salads such as this *yam som-o*, where the tartness of the fruit and the assertiveness of the chillies make for a spicy, refreshing treat. Simply omit the dried shrimp and substitute soy sauce for the fish sauce to make it a perfect vegetarian dish. Pomelos are available in Asian and Chinese supermarkets but if you can't find them, use two grapefruit instead – white grapefruit for tartness or ruby red for a milder, sweeter taste.

serves 4
preparation time: 20 minutes
cooking time: 1 minute

1 large pomelo

2 tablespoons vegetable oil

3 tablespoons finely sliced shallots

3 tablespoons finely sliced garlic

2 small, fresh red Thai chillies, seeded and chopped

3 tablespoons chopped roasted peanuts

3 tablespoons finely shredded spring onions

2 tablespoons chopped dried shrimp

2 tablespoons lime juice

1 tablespoon fish sauce (*nam pla*)

1 tablespoon sugar

a handful of fresh coriander leaves

1 Peel the pomelo and separate the segments, removing any skin or membrane. Gently break the segments into pieces and place in a large bowl.

2 Heat a wok or large frying-pan and add the oil. When it is hot, add the shallots and garlic and stir-fry until golden brown. Remove and drain on kitchen paper.

3 Add the browned shallots and garlic to the pomelo, then add the chillies, peanuts, spring onions and dried shrimp and gently mix together.

4 Combine the lime juice, fish sauce and sugar in a small bowl. Pour this over the pomelo mixture and toss carefully. Garnish with the coriander leaves, arrange on a platter and serve at once.

FISH and SHELLFISH

Thai fish cakes

Nothing could be more tempting than these delicious fish cakes, *thod mun pla*, which are enjoyed by Thais at home, in restaurants and at street stalls all over the country. They come in all shapes and sizes, sometimes formed into balls and poached in soups. Here they are gently fried until crisp, perfumed with the exotic flavours of Thai cookery. Brought forth sizzling from the wok, they make a fine starter, especially when served with a green salad. In Thailand they are often served as part of a main course.

serves 4
preparation time: 30 minutes
cooking time: 15 minutes

450 g (1 lb) skinless white fish fillet, such as cod, sea bass or halibut

2 eggs, beaten

½ teaspoon freshly ground white pepper

1 tablespoon Thai red curry paste

3 kaffir lime leaves, shredded, or 2 tablespoons finely chopped lime zest

2 tablespoons fish sauce (*nam pla*)

1 tablespoon cornflour

2 teaspoons sugar

2 tablespoons chopped fresh coriander

50 g (2 oz) green beans, chopped

450 ml (15 fl oz) groundnut oil, for deep-frying

For the cucumber salad:

450 g (1 lb) cucumbers

3 tablespoons fish sauce (*nam pla*) or light soy sauce

3 tablespoons lime juice

3 tablespoons water

2 tablespoons sugar

1 large, fresh red chilli, seeded and finely sliced

3 tablespoons finely sliced shallots

1 First make the cucumber salad. Peel the cucumbers and slice them lengthways in half, then use a teaspoon to scrape out the seeds. Cut the cucumber halves into thin slices.

2 In a large bowl, combine the fish sauce or soy sauce, lime juice, water and sugar and stir until the sugar has dissolved.

3 Add the cucumber, chilli and shallots and mix well. Leave to stand for at least 20 minutes before serving.

4 Cut the fish fillets into pieces about 2.5 cm (1 in) square. Put the fish, eggs, white pepper and curry paste in a food processor and blend to a smooth paste (if you use a blender, pulse by turning it on and off until the mixture is combined, otherwise the paste will be rubbery).

5 Scrape the mixture into a large bowl and fold in the shredded lime leaves or zest, fish sauce, cornflour, sugar, coriander and green beans.

6 On a floured surface, shape the mixture into round, flat patties about 6 cm (2½ in) in diameter, using a palette knife.

7 Heat a wok or large frying-pan over a high heat and add the oil. When it is very hot and slightly smoking, add a handful of the fish cakes and deep-fry for 3 minutes, until golden and crisp. If the oil gets too hot, reduce the heat slightly. Drain the fish cakes well on kitchen paper and keep warm while you fry the remaining ones. Serve immediately, with the cucumber salad.

Fish with chilli sauce

Freshwater fish of all sorts abound in the lakes and rivers of Thailand. They are usually prepared with pungent sauces, as in this *chuchi pla nuea orn*. But such sauces do not overwhelm their delicate flavour.

serves 4
preparation time: 25 minutes
cooking time: 20 minutes

5 dried red chillies

2 tablespoons vegetable oil

100 g (4 oz) peeled garlic, finely chopped

100 g (4 oz) shallots, finely chopped

1 tablespoon shrimp paste

2 tablespoons fish sauce (*nam pla*) or light soy sauce

2 teaspoons sugar

4 tablespoons water

450 ml (15 fl oz) vegetable oil, for deep-frying

4 small trout, cleaned

plain flour, for dusting

fresh coriander sprigs, to garnish

1 Soak the dried chillies in warm water for about 5 minutes, until softened. Drain well and chop them finely.

2 Heat a wok or large frying-pan over a high heat and add the oil. When it is very hot and slightly smoking, stir in the chillies, garlic, shallots and shrimp paste. Stir-fry for 2 minutes, then add the fish sauce or soy sauce, sugar and water. Remove from the heat and pour the mixture into a bowl.

3 Wipe the wok clean, add the oil for deep-frying and heat. Blot the trout dry inside and out with kitchen paper. Dust the outside thoroughly with flour, shaking off any excess.

4 When the oil is very hot and
slightly smoking, turn the heat
down to medium and fry the
trout for about 4 minutes on
each side, until brown and
crisp (you will probably have to
do this in 2 batches). Remove
the trout and drain on kitchen
paper. Arrange on a platter,
garnish with coriander sprigs
and serve with the chilli sauce.

Crispy fish with mango salad

Pla samlee thod krob gub yam mamuang is a classic combination of flavours and textures. Fresh fish is fried until crisp, then served with a crunchy green mango salad. The results are sensational.

serves 4
preparation time: 20 minutes
cooking time: 5–12 minutes

1 green, unripe mango

2–3 small, fresh red Thai chillies, seeded and shredded

2 tablespoons finely sliced shallots

2 tablespoons lime juice

1 tablespoon fish sauce (*nam pla*)

1 tablespoon sugar

1 x 900 g (2 lb) firm white fish, such as sea bass, cleaned, or 450 g (1 lb) skinless white fish fillet, cut into 4 pieces

plain flour, for dusting

450 ml (15 fl oz) vegetable oil, for deep-frying

3–4 tablespoons crushed roasted peanuts

1 Peel the mango, then cut the flesh off the stone and shred it finely.

2 Mix the shredded mango with the chillies, shallots, lime juice, fish sauce and sugar. Set aside.

3 If you are using a whole fish, score it by making 3 deep cuts on each side. Dry the fish or fish fillets on kitchen paper and dust with flour, shaking off any excess.

4 Heat a wok or large frying-pan over a high heat and add the oil. When it is very hot, add the fish and deep-fry until golden brown; this will take about 10–12 minutes for one large fish or about 5 minutes for fillets. Remove with a fish slice and drain immediately on kitchen paper. Garnish with the crushed peanuts and serve with the mango salad.

Whole fish in coconut milk

In this traditional dish, called *pla tom gathi*, a whole fish is gently steamed to retain its succulence, subtle flavour and delicate texture. It is then paired with an aromatic coconut sauce. Simple steamed rice (see page 17) makes an ideal accompaniment.

Instead of a whole fish you could use 450 g (1 lb) firm white fish fillets, in which case the cooking time should be reduced to about 5 minutes for flat fish such as sole or 8–12 minutes for thicker ones such as cod.

> serves 4
> preparation time: 15 minutes
> cooking time: 1 hour 20 minutes

2 fresh lemon grass stalks

2 tablespoons coarsely chopped fresh galangal or ginger

6 kaffir lime leaves or 2 tablespoons coarsely chopped lime zest

6 fresh coriander roots (optional)

1 x 400 ml (14 fl oz) tin of coconut milk

1 x 900 g (2 lb) firm white fish, such as sea bass, cod or halibut, cleaned

3 tablespoons finely sliced shallots

3 tablespoons fish sauce (*nam pla*)

2 tablespoons lime juice

1 tablespoon sugar

a handful of fresh coriander leaves

1 Peel off the tough outer layers of the lemon grass stalks, leaving the tender whitish centre. Cut it into 7.5 cm (3 in) pieces and crush with the flat of a heavy knife.

2 Put the lemon grass, galangal or ginger, lime leaves or zest, coriander roots, if using, and coconut milk in a pan and bring to the boil. Reduce the heat, then cover and simmer for 1 hour. Strain the liquid, discarding the lemon grass, galangal, lime leaves and coriander roots.

3 Pat the fish dry on kitchen paper and score it on both sides by cutting slashes into the flesh.

4 Set up a steamer or put a rack into a wok or deep pan and fill it with 5 cm (2 in) water. Bring to the boil over a high heat. Put the fish on a deep heatproof plate, pour the coconut mixture on top, then sprinkle over the shallots, fish sauce, lime juice and sugar. Put the plate of fish into the steamer or on the rack. Cover tightly and gently steam the fish for 15–20 minutes, until it is just cooked. Remove from the steamer, garnish with coriander leaves and serve at once.

Stir-fried squid with chilli and basil

Thai chefs are masters with seafood, especially squid. This aromatic stir-fried dish, *pla muk phat bai krapao*, is one of the simplest to cook and is flavoured with chillies, basil and garlic – a mixture that is the essence of Thai cooking.

Once the squid has been prepared, the dish is only minutes away from completion. For maximum impact, delay the final cooking until the last possible moment.

serves 4
preparation time: 30 minutes
cooking time: 10 minutes

675 g (1½ lb) fresh squid (or 450 g (1 lb) cleaned frozen squid, thawed)

175 g (6 oz) fresh or frozen petits pois

1½ tablespoons vegetable oil

4 tablespoons coarsely chopped garlic

3 tablespoons finely sliced shallots

2–3 small, fresh red Thai chillies, seeded and chopped

1 tablespoon fish sauce (*nam pla*)

2 tablespoons oyster sauce

2 teaspoons sugar

a handful of fresh Thai basil leaves or ordinary basil leaves

1 Pull the head and tentacles of the squid away from the body; the intestines should come away with them. Then pull off the thin, purplish skin.

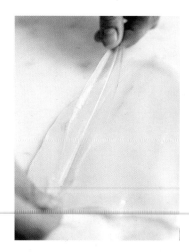

2 Using a small, sharp knife, slit the body open; remove and discard the transparent bony section. Wash the body thoroughly under cold running water and cut it into 4 cm (1½ in) strips.

3 Slice the tentacles off the head, cutting just above the eye (you may also have to remove the polyp, or beak, from the centre of the ring of tentacles). Discard the head and reserve the tentacles.

4 If you are using fresh peas, blanch them for 3 minutes in boiling salted water, then drain and set aside. If you are using frozen peas, simply thaw them and set them aside.

5 Heat a wok or large frying-pan over a high heat and add the oil. When it is very hot and slightly smoking, add the garlic and stir-fry for 1 minute, until lightly browned. Remove with a slotted spoon and drain on kitchen paper.

6 Add the squid strips and tentacles to the wok and stir-fry for 1 minute, until beginning to turn opaque.

7 Add the shallots, chillies, peas, fish sauce, oyster sauce and sugar and stir-fry for 3 minutes. Toss in the basil and give one last stir. Turn the mixture on to a platter, garnish with the fried garlic and serve at once.

Red curry prawns

This is a tasty version of a classic Thai dish, *gaeng phed ghoong*. Once the sauce is made, the prawns cook in just minutes. Serve with plain steamed rice (see page 17).

serves 4
preparation time: 20 minutes
cooking time: 20 minutes

1½ tablespoons vegetable oil

3 tablespoons coarsely chopped garlic

2 tablespoons finely sliced shallots

2 teaspoons cumin seeds

1 teaspoon shrimp paste

1½ tablespoons Thai red curry paste

1 x 400 ml (14 fl oz) tin of coconut milk

1 tablespoon fish sauce (*nam pla*) or light soy sauce

2 teaspoons sugar

a small handful of fresh Thai basil leaves or ordinary basil leaves, shredded

4 kaffir lime leaves or 1 table-spoon shredded lime zest

450 g (1 lb) raw prawns, shelled and de-veined (see page 15)

a handful of fresh coriander leaves

1 Heat a wok or large frying-pan until it is very hot and add the oil. When it is hot, add the garlic, shallots and cumin seeds and stir-fry for 5 minutes or until well toasted. Then add the shrimp paste and curry paste and stir-fry for 2 minutes.

2 Now add the coconut milk, fish sauce or soy sauce, sugar, basil leaves and lime leaves or zest. Reduce the heat and simmer for 5 minutes.

3 Add the prawns and cook for
   5 minutes, stirring from time
   to time. Add the coriander
   leaves and give the mixture
   a good stir, then serve.

Green curry prawns

This delectable dish is quick and easy to make. The fiery green curry is mellowed by the rich sweetness of coconut milk. It makes a wonderful meal when served with plain steamed rice (see page 17). In Thailand, it is known as *gaeng kheow wan ghoong*.

serves 4
preparation time: 15 minutes
cooking time: 15 minutes

1 fresh lemon grass stalk

1½ tablespoons vegetable oil

2 tablespoons Thai green curry paste

4 kaffir lime leaves, torn, or 1 tablespoon shredded lime zest

2 tablespoons fish sauce (*nam pla*) or light soy sauce

2 teaspoons sugar

1 x 400 ml (14 fl oz) tin of coconut milk

450 g (1 lb) raw prawns, shelled and de-veined (see page 15)

a small handful of fresh Thai basil leaves or ordinary basil leaves, shredded

1 Peel off the tough outer layers of the lemon grass stalk, leaving the tender whitish centre, and slice it finely.

2 Heat a wok or large frying-pan until it is very hot and add the oil. Now add the green curry paste and stir-fry for 2 minutes.

4 Add the prawns and cook for 5 minutes, stirring from time to time. Add the basil leaves and give the mixture a good stir, then serve.

3 Add the lemon grass, lime leaves or zest, fish sauce or soy sauce, sugar and coconut milk. Reduce the heat and simmer for 5 minutes.

Braised clams with chilli and basil

This is one of the easiest Thai recipes. Clams cook quickly and have an assertive seafood flavour, made even more distinctive here by the addition of fresh basil and chillies. If clams are unavailable, you could substitute mussels and the dish will be just as delectable. Its Thai name is *hoy lai phad prik*.

serves 4
preparation time: 20 minutes
cooking time: 7 minutes

1 kg (2¼ lb) fresh clams

1½ tablespoons vegetable oil

3 tablespoons coarsely chopped garlic

2 tablespoons finely chopped shallots

3 large, fresh red or green chillies, seeded and shredded

2 tablespoons fish sauce (*nam pla*) or light soy sauce

a handful of fresh Thai basil leaves or ordinary basil leaves

1 Scrub the clams under cold running water, discarding any open ones that do not close when tapped lightly on a work surface.

2 Heat a wok or large frying-pan over a high heat and add the oil. When it is very hot and slightly smoking, add the garlic, shallots, chillies and clams and stir-fry them for 3–4 minutes, until the clams begin to open.

3 Add the fish sauce or soy sauce, then reduce the heat, cover the pan and cook for 3 minutes. Stir in the basil leaves and serve at once.

Coconut mussels

Thais love any food from the sea, and no wonder: seafood dishes are easy to prepare and if you add exotic Thai seasonings they become a delicious treat. What could be simpler than this recipe made with mussels? You will find this dish, known as *hoy malaeng pooh gathi*, a satisfying fish course that cooks up in minutes – ideal for a crowd.

serves 4–6
preparation time: 25 minutes
cooking time: 10 minutes

1.5 kg (3 lb) fresh mussels

2 fresh lemon grass stalks

1 x 400 ml (14 fl oz) tin of coconut milk

3 tablespoons water

3 kaffir lime leaves or 1 tablespoon shredded lime zest

2 tablespoons coarsely chopped spring onions

1 tablespoon Thai green curry paste

3 tablespoons chopped coriander roots or stalks

2 tablespoons fish sauce (*nam pla*)

1 teaspoon sugar

a large handful of fresh Thai basil leaves or ordinary basil leaves, shredded

1 Scrub the mussels under cold running water and scrape off any barnacles with a small knife. Pull out and discard the fibrous 'beards'. Discard any open mussels that don't close when tapped lightly on a work surface.

2 Peel off the tough outer layers of the lemon grass stalks, leaving the tender whitish centre. Cut it into 7.5 cm (3 in) pieces and crush with the flat of a heavy knife.

3 Pour the coconut milk and water into a wok or large frying-pan. Add the lemon grass, lime leaves or zest, spring onions, curry paste, coriander roots or stalks, fish sauce and sugar and bring to a simmer.

4 Add the mussels, then cover and cook over a high heat for 5 minutes, until all the mussels have opened (discard any that remain closed). Give the mixture a final stir, add the basil leaves and serve at once.

Seafood in coconut milk

Thailand enjoys a bountiful supply of seafood from her long coastline, leading to an abundance of relatively inexpensive fish and shellfish dishes such as this one, known as *hor mok talay*. Bracing seasonings and rich coconut milk bring out the best in seafood. Like the Thais, use whatever is freshest on the day you are cooking.

serves 4–6
preparation time: 30 minutes
cooking time: 15 minutes

1.5–1.6 kg (3–3½ lb) freshly cooked crab in the shell

175 g (6 oz) fresh mussels

3 fresh lemon grass stalks

4 garlic cloves, crushed

4 tablespoons finely sliced shallots

3 tablespoons chopped fresh coriander

2 small, fresh red or green Thai chillies, seeded and chopped

1 tablespoon black peppercorns

2 teaspoons shredded lime zest

2 x 400 ml (14 fl oz) tins of coconut milk

175 g (6 oz) raw unshelled prawns

175 g (6 oz) fresh scallops with roe

2 tablespoons fish sauce (*nam pla*)

2 tablespoons lime juice

2 tablespoons sugar

1 Remove the tail flap, stomach sac and feathery gills from the cooked crab, if necessary. Using a heavy knife or cleaver, cut the crab, shell included, into large pieces.

2 Scrub the mussels under cold running water and scrape off any barnacles with a small knife. Pull out and discard the fibrous 'beards'. Discard any open mussels that don't close when tapped lightly on a work surface.

3 Peel off the tough outer layers of the lemon grass stalks, leaving the tender whitish centre. Chop it finely and place in a blender with the garlic, shallots, coriander, chillies, black peppercorns and lime zest. Add about 3 tablespoons of the coconut milk and blend to a paste.

5 Add the crab, mussels, prawns, scallops, fish sauce, lime juice and sugar, then cover and simmer for 10 minutes. Turn the mixture on to a large platter and serve. It is perfectly good manners to eat the crab, prawns and mussels with your fingers, but I suggest that you have a bowl of water decorated with lemon slices on the table so that your guests can rinse their fingers.

4 Pour the remaining coconut milk into a wok or deep pan and bring to the boil. Reduce the heat, stir in the blended spice paste and simmer for 3 minutes.

MEAT and POULTRY

Red pork curry

Gaeng phed moo is a quick and easy Thai curry. The assertive spices and seasonings enhance this classic treatment for pork.

serves 4
preparation time: 10 minutes
cooking time: 10 minutes

450 g (1 lb) pork fillet

1½ tablespoons vegetable oil

2 tablespoons Thai red curry paste

3 tablespoons finely shredded fresh galangal or ginger

1 teaspoon ground turmeric

2 tablespoons finely sliced garlic

1 x 400 ml (14 fl oz) tin of coconut milk

2 tablespoons fish sauce (*nam pla*)

4 kaffir lime leaves or 1 tablespoon shredded lime zest

2 teaspoons sugar

a handful of fresh Thai basil leaves or ordinary basil leaves

1 Cut the pork into thin slices about 5 cm (2 in) long and set aside.

2 Heat a wok or large frying-pan over a medium heat and add the oil. When it is hot, add the curry paste and stir-fry for 30 seconds. Add the pork slices, turn up the heat and stir-fry them for 1 minute or until they are entirely coated with the curry paste. Remove with a slotted spoon and set aside.

3 Add the galangal or ginger, turmeric and garlic to the wok and stir-fry for 10 seconds. Stir in the coconut milk, fish sauce, lime leaves or zest and sugar, bring to the boil and simmer for 5 minutes.

4 Return the pork to the sauce and simmer for 3 minutes or until it is cooked through. Toss in the basil and give it a final stir. Serve at once.

Pork with shrimp paste

In this dish called *moo phad gapi*, tender pork fillet is marinated in dark soy sauce and flavoured with aromatic shrimp paste to make a special Thai treat. Serve with your favourite stir-fried vegetable dish and plain steamed rice (see page 17) for a satisfying meal.

serves 4
preparation time: 10 minutes,
  plus 20 minutes' marinating
cooking time: 6 minutes

450 g (1 lb) pork fillet

1 teaspoon salt

1 tablespoon dark soy sauce

1½ tablespoons vegetable oil

2 small, fresh red or green Thai chillies, seeded and chopped

1 small onion, coarsely chopped

2 tablespoons finely sliced shallots

2 tablespoons fish sauce (*nam pla*)

1 tablespoon light soy sauce

½ teaspoon freshly ground white pepper

1 teaspoon sugar

1½ teaspoons shrimp paste

a handful of fresh coriander leaves

1 Cut the pork into thin slices about 4 cm (1½ in) long and place in a bowl. Add the salt and the dark soy sauce, mix well and leave to marinate for 20 minutes.

2 Heat a wok or large frying-pan over a high heat until it is very hot, then add the oil. When it is very hot and slightly smoking, add the marinated pork and stir-fry for about 2 minutes. Remove with a slotted spoon and drain in a colander.

4 Return the drained pork to the wok and stir-fry for 2 minutes or until the pork is cooked through. Add the coriander leaves, give the mixture a good stir and serve at once.

3 Quickly add the chillies, onion and shallots to the wok and stir-fry for 2 minutes. Then add the fish sauce, light soy sauce, white pepper, sugar and shrimp paste.

Mussaman-style beef curry

This delicious and inviting recipe (*mussaman nuea*) has its roots in the Middle East but travelled to Thailand with the spread of the Muslim religion. Thai tolerance of foreign influences has allowed cooks to add their own flavours to this savoury curry. Try to find Mussaman curry paste; it is well worth the search.

serves 4–6
preparation time: 15 minutes
cooking time: 2¼ hours

2 tablespoons vegetable oil

1.5 kg (3 lb) stewing beef, such as brisket or shin, cut into 5 cm (2 in) cubes

3 tablespoons Mussaman curry paste (or Madras curry paste)

225 g (8 oz) small new potatoes, peeled

3 tablespoons chopped roasted peanuts

a handful of fresh coriander leaves

For the braising sauce:

2 fresh lemon grass stalks

1.2 litres (2 pints) tinned coconut milk

600 ml (1 pint) hot water

3 tablespoons brown or white sugar

3 tablespoons fish sauce (*nam pla*) or light soy sauce

2 tablespoons lime juice

2 teaspoons shrimp paste

3 tablespoons finely sliced shallots

2 cinnamon sticks

6 cardamom pods

¼ teaspoon freshly grated nutmeg

4 kaffir lime leaves or 1 tablespoon shredded lime zest

1 Heat a wok or large frying-pan and add the oil. When it is very hot and slightly smoking, add the beef and fry for about 10 minutes, until it is brown all over (you will need to do this in 2 or 3 batches).

2 Pour off any excess fat, leaving 1 tablespoon of oil in the pan. Put all the meat back in the pan, add the Mussaman curry paste and stir-fry with the beef for about 5 minutes. Transfer this mixture to a large casserole or pot.

3 For the sauce, peel off the tough outer layers of the lemon grass stalks, leaving the tender whitish centre. Cut it into 7.5 cm (3 in) pieces, crush with the flat of a heavy knife, then add to the casserole with all the rest of the braising sauce ingredients. Bring to the boil, skim off any fat from the surface and turn the heat as low as possible. Cover and braise for 1 hour.

4 Add the potatoes to the casserole and cook for another 30 minutes or until the meat is quite tender. Then remove the lid, turn the heat up to high and boil rapidly for about 15 minutes to reduce and thicken the sauce. Garnish with the chopped peanuts and coriander before serving.

Stir-fried minced pork with basil

This simple family dish, called *moo phad bai horapa*, is quick and easy to make. The basil is the key to its success. Its fresh green colour, distinctive aroma and unique flavour work to make something very Thai and very special. Serve with rice or noodles and a vegetable.

serves 2–4
preparation time: 10 minutes
cooking time: 10 minutes

1½ tablespoons vegetable oil

1 tablespoon Thai red curry paste

3 tablespoons coarsely chopped garlic

3 tablespoons finely sliced shallots

450 g (1 lb) minced pork

2 tablespoons fish sauce (*nam pla*)

3 tablespoons coconut milk

2 teaspoons sugar

a very large handful of fresh Thai basil leaves or ordinary basil leaves, chopped

1 Heat a wok or large frying-pan over a medium heat and add the oil. When it is very hot and slightly smoking, add the curry paste and stir-fry gently for 1 minute, until it begins to melt.

2 Add the garlic and shallots and stir-fry for a minute longer. Then add the pork and stir-fry for 3 minutes.

3 Now add the fish sauce, coconut milk and sugar and stir-fry for 3 minutes longer. Finally, add the chopped basil and stir-fry for another minute. Serve at once.

Fragrant Thai meatballs

Walking through Bangkok, one is always pleasantly aware of exotic, mouthwatering aromas emanating from the many small restaurants and street stalls that line the thoroughfares. These meatballs are typical Thai street food. What makes them so deliciously savoury is the spices blending into the succulent beef and pork, while the egg white gives them a delicate, light texture. They are very easy to prepare and make an excellent party snack with drinks, or serve them with other dishes for a main course. Their Thai name is *look chin moo rue nuea*.

serves 4
preparation time: 20 minutes
cooking time: 8 minutes

100 g (4 oz) minced beef

100 g (4 oz) minced fatty pork

1 egg white

2 tablespoons very cold water

1 teaspoon salt

½ teaspoon freshly ground black pepper

2 tablespoons finely chopped garlic

3 tablespoons finely chopped fresh coriander

2 tablespoons finely chopped spring onions

1 tablespoon fish sauce (*nam pla*)

2 teaspoons sugar

plain flour for dusting

450 ml (15 fl oz) vegetable oil, for deep-frying

1 Blitz the beef and pork in a food processor for a few seconds. Slowly add the egg white and cold water and process for a few more seconds, until they are fully incorporated into the meat.

2 Add all the remaining ingredients except the flour and vegetable oil and process for about a minute, until the mixture becomes a light paste.

3 Using your hands, shape the mixture into about ten 4 cm (1½ in) balls. Dust them evenly with flour, shaking off any excess. The meatballs will be quite fragile and soft.

4 Heat a wok or large frying-pan over a high heat and add the oil. When it is very hot and slightly smoking, gently drop in as many meatballs as will fit easily in one layer. Fry for about 4 minutes, adjusting the heat as necessary, until they are crisp and browned all over and cooked through. Remove with a slotted spoon and drain on kitchen paper. Serve at once.

Green chicken curry

Gaeng kheow wan gai is one of the best-known Thai dishes and it has captivated Western palates. It is easy to see why. The richness of the coconut milk combined with green curry paste and chicken is a winning combination. It makes a satisfying main course served with steamed rice (see page 17).

serves 4
preparation time: 15 minutes
cooking time: 20 minutes

450 g (1 lb) boneless, skinless chicken thighs

2 fresh lemon grass stalks

1½ tablespoons vegetable oil

2–3 tablespoons Thai green curry paste

3 tablespoons finely sliced shallots

3 tablespoons coarsely chopped garlic

1 tablespoon finely chopped fresh galangal or ginger

4 kaffir lime leaves or 2 teaspoons shredded lime zest

1 tablespoon fish sauce (*nam pla*)

2 teaspoons sugar

1 teaspoon salt

225 g (8 oz) pea aubergines, left whole, or ordinary aubergines cut into 2.5 cm (1 in) chunks

1 x 400 ml (14 fl oz) tin of coconut milk

3 tablespoons water

a small handful of fresh coriander leaves

a large handful of fresh Thai basil leaves or ordinary basil leaves

1 Cut the chicken into 2.5 cm (1 in) chunks. Peel off the tough outer layers of the lemon grass stalks, leaving the tender whitish centre, and chop it finely.

2 Heat a wok or large frying-pan until it is very hot and add the oil. Add the green curry paste and stir-fry for 2 minutes, then add the chicken and mix until it is coated with the paste.

3 Now add the lemon grass, shallots, garlic, galangal or ginger, lime leaves or zest, fish sauce, sugar and salt and stir-fry for another minute.

4 Add the aubergines and pour in the coconut milk and water. Turn the heat to low and simmer for 15 minutes or until the chicken is cooked through. Add the coriander and basil leaves, give the mixture a good stir and serve at once.

Red chicken curry

Gaeng phed gai is a slightly different version of Thai chicken curry from the previous one, using red curry paste. It is just as delicious as its green counterpart but perhaps less well known in the West. You will love its rich, savoury flavours.

serves 4
preparation time: 15 minutes
cooking time: 20 minutes

450 g (1 lb) boneless, skinless chicken thighs

2 fresh lemon grass stalks

1½ tablespoons vegetable oil

2–3 tablespoons Thai red curry paste

225 g (8 oz) small potatoes, peeled

3 tablespoons finely sliced shallots

3 tablespoons coarsely chopped garlic

1 tablespoon finely chopped fresh galangal or ginger

4 kaffir lime leaves or 2 teaspoons shredded lime zest

1 tablespoon fish sauce (*nam pla*)

2 teaspoons sugar

1 teaspoon salt

1 x 400 ml (14 fl oz) tin of coconut milk

3 tablespoons water

a large handful of fresh coriander leaves

50 g (2 oz) roasted peanuts, crushed

1 large, fresh red chilli, seeded and shredded

1 Cut the chicken into 2.5 cm (1 in) chunks. Peel off the tough outer layers of the lemon grass stalks, leaving the tender whitish centre, and chop it finely.

2 Heat a wok or large frying-pan until it is very hot and add the oil. Add the red curry paste and stir-fry for 2 minutes, then add the chicken and potatoes and mix until they are coated with the paste.

3 Add the lemon grass, shallots, garlic, galangal or ginger, lime leaves or zest, fish sauce, sugar and salt and stir-fry for another minute.

4 Pour in the coconut milk and water, turn the heat to low and simmer for 15 minutes or until the chicken is cooked through. Add the coriander, stir and garnish with the chopped peanuts and chilli. Serve at once.

Stir-fried chicken with chillies and basil

This traditional dish, called *gai phad bai krapao*, is very easy to prepare. The unique, pungent aroma of Thai basil makes it especially mouthwatering.

serves 4
preparation time: 10 minutes
cooking time: 20 minutes

450 g (1 lb) boneless, skinless chicken thighs

2 tablespoons vegetable oil

3 tablespoons finely sliced shallots

3 tablespoons coarsely chopped garlic

3 fresh red or green Thai chillies, seeded and finely shredded

2 tablespoons fish sauce (*nam pla*)

2 teaspoons dark soy sauce

2 teaspoons sugar

a large handful of Thai or ordinary basil leaves

1 Cut the chicken into 2.5 cm (1 in) chunks. Heat a wok or large frying-pan until it is very hot, then add 1 tablespoon of the oil. When it is very hot, add the chicken and stir-fry over a high heat for 8 minutes, until browned all over. Using a slotted spoon, transfer the chicken to a colander.

2 Reheat the wok and add the remaining oil. Toss in the shallots and garlic and stir-fry for 3 minutes, until they are golden brown.

3 Return the chicken to the wok and add the chillies, fish sauce, dark soy sauce and sugar. Stir-fry over a high heat for 8 minutes or until the chicken is cooked through. Stir in the basil leaves and serve at once.

Thai barbecue chicken

The streets of Thailand are redolent with the aromas of smoky grilled foods. One of the most popular dishes is *gai yang*, a tasty version of barbecue chicken. It is made using chicken thighs, which are not only meatier than chicken breasts but tend to stay moist despite the intense heat of the grill. The secret is to marinate the chicken overnight. Once that is done, the rest is quite easy. It makes a memorable picnic dish or summer meal, served at room temperature.

serves 4
preparation time: 10 minutes,
  plus marinating overnight
cooking time: 20 minutes

900 g (2 lb) chicken thighs, with bone in

a handful of fresh coriander sprigs

For the marinade:

2 tablespoons fish sauce (*nam pla*)

3 tablespoons coarsely chopped garlic

3 tablespoons chopped fresh coriander

2 small, fresh Thai red or green chillies, seeded and chopped

4 kaffir lime leaves or 1 tablespoon lime zest

2 teaspoons sugar

1 tablespoon Shaoxing rice wine or dry sherry

1 teaspoon ground turmeric

2 teaspoons Thai red curry paste

1 teaspoon salt

½ teaspoon freshly ground black pepper

4 tablespoons tinned coconut milk

1 Purée all the marinade ingredients together in a blender (or pound them together in a mortar and pestle).

2 Blot the chicken thighs dry on kitchen paper. Put them in a large bowl, add the marinade and mix well. Cover with cling film and leave to marinate in the fridge overnight. The next day, remove the chicken from the fridge and leave at room temperature for 40 minutes before cooking. Light a barbecue or preheat the grill to high. When the charcoal is ash white or the grill is very hot, grill the thighs for 10 minutes on each side or until cooked through.

3 Place on a platter, garnish with the coriander sprigs and serve immediately, or allow to cool and serve at room temperature.

Chicken in pandan leaves

This is a version of one of my favourite Thai recipes, *gai hor bai toey*. The chicken is marinated, then wrapped in fragrant pandan leaves and fried, which releases the nut-like flavour of the leaves. It makes a wonderful party dish for a large crowd. Pandan leaves are similar to bamboo leaves and are stocked by some Asian and Chinese supermarkets. If you cannot find them, just use aluminium foil.

serves 4–6
preparation time: 40 minutes,
  plus marinating overnight
cooking time: 30 minutes

450 g (1 lb) boneless, skinless chicken thighs

40 pandan leaves, cut into 12.5 cm (5 in) squares

600 ml (1 pint) vegetable oil, for deep-frying

For the marinade:

2 tablespoons light soy sauce

3 tablespoons coarsely chopped garlic

2 tablespoons oyster sauce

2 teaspoons sugar

2 tablespoons finely chopped coriander root or fresh coriander

1 tablespoon fish sauce (*nam pla*)

2 teaspoons sesame oil

½ teaspoon freshly ground black pepper

For the sauce:

25 ml (1 fl oz) white rice vinegar or cider vinegar

2 tablespoons dark soy sauce

2 teaspoons sugar

2 teaspoons roasted sesame seeds

1 small, fresh red Thai chilli, seeded and finely chopped

1 Put all the marinade ingredients in a blender and process to a smooth purée.

2 Cut the chicken into bite-sized pieces. Put them in a large bowl, add the marinade and mix well. Cover with cling film and leave to marinate in the fridge overnight.

3 When you are ready to cook the chicken, remove it from the fridge and wrap a piece in each pandan leaf (or in a foil square).

4 If your pandan leaves are small you may have to use more than one, overlapping each other. Tie each parcel with string, or secure with bamboo skewers.

5 Put all the ingredients for the sauce in a bowl and whisk them together, then set aside.

6 Heat a wok or large, deep frying-pan until very hot, then add the vegetable oil. When it is hot and slightly smoking, add the chicken parcels, 5 at a time, and fry for about 4 minutes, until cooked through. Drain thoroughly on kitchen paper and keep warm while you fry the remaining parcels. Serve immediately, with the sauce.

VEGETABLES and SIDE DISHES

Stir-fried mixed vegetables

This is a colourful and nutritious offering. An assortment of vegetables is suggested below but you may choose your own favourites. When stir-frying, remember to begin with the firmer vegetables, which will need more cooking. This dish is known as *phad phag ruam mit* in Thailand.

To make this a vegetarian dish, simply use vegetarian oyster sauce (which is made with mushrooms) and substitute light soy sauce for the fish sauce.

serves 4
preparation time: 15 minutes
cooking time: 10 minutes

225 g (8 oz) broccoli

225 g (8 oz) asparagus

225 g (8 oz) Chinese leaves (Peking cabbage)

225 g (8 oz) fresh or tinned baby sweetcorn

2 tablespoons vegetable oil

3 tablespoons finely sliced garlic

3 tablespoons finely sliced shallots

2 small, fresh red Thai chillies, seeded and sliced

1½ tablespoons fish sauce (*nam pla*)

2 tablespoons oyster sauce

2 teaspoons sugar

1 teaspoon salt

1 Divide the broccoli into florets. Peel the stalks and slice them thinly on the diagonal. Trim the woody ends of the asparagus and then cut into 4 cm (1½ in) lengths. Cut the Chinese leaves into 4 cm (1½ in) strips.

2 Blanch the sweetcorn and broccoli in a large pan of boiling salted water for 3 minutes. Drain well and then plunge them into cold water to stop them cooking further.

3 Heat a wok or large frying-pan over a high heat until it is medium hot. Add the oil and garlic and stir-fry for 1–1½ minutes, until the garlic is golden brown. Remove with a slotted spoon and place on kitchen paper to drain. Now add the shallots and chillies to the wok and stir-fry for 1 minute.

4 Add the corn and asparagus and stir-fry for 30 seconds. Add the fish sauce and bring the mixture to the boil, then cover and cook over a high heat for 2 minutes.

5 Add the broccoli and Chinese leaves, together with the oyster sauce, sugar and salt. Continue cooking over a high heat for 3 minutes or until the vegetables are tender. Turn on to a platter, garnish with the fried garlic and serve at once.

Sweet and sour aubergines

This easy dish, called *yam makhua*, makes a delectable accompaniment to any meal. If you substitute light soy sauce for the fish sauce it will be quite suitable for vegetarians.

serves 2–4
preparation time: 15 minutes,
  plus at least 30 minutes' draining
cooking time: 30–40 minutes

450 g (1 lb) aubergines

3 tablespoons finely sliced shallots

2 tablespoons fish sauce (*nam pla*) or light soy sauce

2 tablespoons lime juice

1 tablespoon sugar

a handful of fresh coriander leaves

1 Preheat the oven to 240°C/475°F/Gas Mark 9. Using a sharp knife, prick the skin of the aubergines. Place them in a roasting tin and bake for 30–40 minutes, until they are soft. Leave to cool.

2 Peel the aubergines, then put them in a colander and leave to drain for at least 30 minutes. Dice them and place in a bowl (this can all be done several hours in advance).

3 Put the shallots, fish sauce or soy sauce, lime juice and sugar in a saucepan and bring to a simmer. Pour this mixture over the aubergines and mix well. Garnish with the coriander leaves and serve.

Classic Thai fried rice

Fried rice is found everywhere in Thailand. It is often served with a fried egg on top, which makes it a meal on its own. Its Thai name is *khao phad ruam mit*.

serves 4–6
preparation time: 15 minutes, plus preparing the rice at least 2 hours in advance
cooking time: 10 minutes

Enough long-grain white rice to fill a measuring jug to 400 ml (14 fl oz)

2 eggs, beaten

2 teaspoons sesame oil

½ teaspoon salt

225 g (8 oz) boneless, skinless chicken breasts

2 tablespoons vegetable oil

2 tablespoons coarsely chopped garlic

1 small onion, finely chopped

½ teaspoon freshly ground black pepper

3 tablespoons fish sauce (*nam pla*)

3 tablespoons finely chopped spring onions

3 tablespoons finely chopped fresh coriander

2 small, fresh red or green Thai chillies, seeded and chopped

To garnish:

1 lime, cut into wedges

4 fried eggs (optional)

1 At least 2 hours in advance, or the night before, cook the rice according to the instructions on page 17. Spread it out on a baking tray and allow it to cool thoroughly, then put it in the refrigerator.

2 Beat the eggs with the sesame oil and salt and set aside. Cut the chicken into 1 cm (½ in) dice.

3 Heat a wok or large frying-pan over a high heat and add the oil. When it is very hot and slightly smoking, add the garlic, onion and black pepper and stir-fry for 2 minutes. Then add the chicken and stir-fry for another 2 minutes. Add the cold cooked rice and continue to stir-fry for 3 minutes.

4 Add the fish sauce, spring onions, coriander and chillies and stir-fry for 2 minutes.

5 Finally, add the egg mixture and continue to stir-fry for another minute. Turn on to a platter, garnish with the lime wedges and the fried eggs, if using, and serve at once.

Vegetarian fried rice

Buddhism is a powerful force in Thai culture. For one week in autumn, Thais celebrate by eating only vegetables to purify both body and soul. *Khao phad jay* is a typical vegetarian dish one would find during this popular festival.

serves 4–6

preparation time: 15 minutes, plus preparing the rice at least 2 hours in advance

cooking time: 12 minutes

Enough long-grain white rice to fill a measuring jug to 400 ml (14 fl oz)

2 tablespoons vegetable oil

3 tablespoons coarsely chopped garlic

1 small onion, finely chopped

½ teaspoon freshly ground black pepper

175 g (6 oz) runner beans or French beans, diced

100 g (4 oz) fresh or frozen sweetcorn

2 tablespoons light soy sauce

2 teaspoons Thai green curry paste

To garnish:

3 spring onions

1 cucumber

1 lime

1 At least 2 hours in advance, or the night before, cook the rice according to the instructions on page 17. Spread it out on a baking tray and allow it to cool thoroughly, then put it in the refrigerator.

2 Prepare the garnishes: cut the spring onions on a slight diagonal into 2.5 cm (1 in) lengths. Peel the cucumber, then slice it in half lengthways and remove the seeds with a teaspoon. Cut the cucumber into very thin slices. Cut the lime into wedges. Set aside.

3 Heat a wok or large frying-pan over a high heat and add the oil. When it is very hot and slightly smoking, add the garlic, onion and black pepper and stir-fry for 2 minutes. Then add the beans and sweetcorn and continue to stir-fry for 3 minutes.

4 Add the cold cooked rice and stir-fry for 5 minutes. Finally, add the light soy sauce and curry paste and stir-fry for 2 minutes. Turn on to a platter, garnish with the spring onions, cucumber slices and lime wedges and serve at once.

Coconut rice

For a real vegetarian treat, this rich rice dish, called *khao mun*, is sometimes served with Spicy papaya salad (see page 40).

Enough long-grain white rice
   to fill a measuring jug to
   400 ml (14 fl oz)

1 x 400 ml (14 fl oz) tin of
   coconut milk

300 ml (10 fl oz) water

½ teaspoon salt

1 teaspoon sugar

> serves 4
>
> preparation time: 5 minutes, plus
>   10 minutes for the rice to rest
>
> cooking time: 15 minutes

1 Put the rice into a large bowl and wash it in several changes of water until the water becomes clear.

2 Drain the rice and put it into a heavy-based pan with the coconut milk, water, salt and sugar. Bring to a simmer, then turn the heat as low as possible, cover the pan with a very tight-fitting lid and let the rice cook undisturbed for 15 minutes.

3 Remove from the heat. Leave the rice to rest, covered, for 10 minutes, then serve. You will notice the bottom of the rice is lightly browned – this is normal and actually tastes quite delicious.

Chicken fried rice with basil

Fried rice in all its forms is a favourite in Thailand. *Khao phad gai horapa* is one of the most popular versions, made easily with chicken and fragrant basil. Use Thai jasmine rice, if possible, as its aroma adds so much to the dish.

serves 4–6
preparation time: 15 minutes,
   plus preparing the rice at least
   2 hours in advance
cooking time: 10 minutes

Enough Thai jasmine rice or long-grain white rice to fill a measuring jug to 400 ml (14 fl oz)

225 g (8 oz) boneless, skin-less chicken breasts

2 tablespoons vegetable oil

3 tablespoons finely sliced garlic

1 small onion, finely chopped

3 tablespoons sliced shallots

100 g (4 oz) large, fresh red chillies, seeded and shredded

2 teaspoons salt

½ teaspoon freshly ground black pepper

2 teaspoons sugar

1 tablespoon fish sauce (*nam pla*)

a handful of fresh Thai basil leaves or ordinary basil leaves

3 tablespoons finely shredded spring onions

1 At least 2 hours in advance, or the night before, cook the rice according to the instructions on page 17. Spread it out on a baking tray and allow it to cool thoroughly, then put it in the refrigerator.

2 Slice the chicken into thin strips and set aside. Heat a wok or large frying-pan over a high heat and add the oil. When it is very hot and slightly smoking, add the garlic, onion, shallots, chillies, salt and black pepper and stir-fry for 2 minutes.

3 Add the chicken and stir-fry for 2 minutes, then add the rice and continue to stir-fry for 3 minutes. Add the sugar and fish sauce and stir-fry for 2 minutes.

4 Finally, add the basil leaves and stir-fry for another minute. Turn on to a platter, garnish with the spring onions and serve hot – or leave to cool and serve as a rice salad.

Stir-fried rice noodles

Phad thai is probably one of the most popular dishes in Thailand, prepared in homes throughout the country as well as at countless street stalls. It combines the essential Thai flavours of sweet, sour, hot and spicy. The garnishes are mixed in just before serving.

serves 4
preparation time: 25 minutes,
 plus 25 minutes' soaking
cooking time: 10 minutes

225 g (8 oz) wide dried rice noodles

3 tablespoons vegetable oil

450 g (1 lb) raw prawns, shelled and de-veined (see page 15)

3 tablespoons coarsely chopped garlic

3 tablespoons finely sliced shallots

2 large, fresh red or green chillies, seeded and chopped

2 eggs, beaten

2 tablespoons lime juice

3 tablespoons fish sauce (*nam pla*)

1 tablespoon Sweet chilli sauce (see page 42)

1 teaspoon sugar

½ teaspoon freshly ground black pepper

175 g (6 oz) bean sprouts

To garnish:

1 lime, cut into wedges

3 tablespoons coarsely chopped fresh coriander

3 spring onions, sliced

3 tablespoons coarsely chopped roasted peanuts

1 teaspoon dried chilli flakes

1 Soak the rice noodles in a bowl of warm water for 25 minutes, then drain them in a colander or sieve.

2 Heat a wok or large frying-pan over a high heat until it is very hot, then add 1 table-spoon of the oil. When it is very hot and slightly smoking, add the prawns and stir-fry for about 2 minutes. Remove from the pan and set aside.

3 Reheat the wok, add the remaining oil, then add the garlic, shallots and chillies and stir-fry for 1 minute. Now add the drained noodles and stir-fry for another minute. Finally, add the beaten eggs, lime juice, fish sauce, chilli sauce, sugar and black pepper and continue to stir-fry for 3 minutes.

4 Return the prawns to the wok, toss in the bean sprouts and stir-fry for 2 minutes. Turn the mixture on to a platter, garnish with the lime wedges, coriander, spring onions, peanuts and chilli flakes and serve at once.

STIR-FRIED RICE NOODLES | 115

Spicy noodle salad

Yam woon sen is one of many culinary delights found in night markets throughout Thailand. It can be cooked in the wok in just minutes. These delectable dishes are often served at room temperature.

serves 4
preparation time: 10 minutes,
 plus 25 minutes' soaking
cooking time: 8 minutes

225 g (8 oz) flat rice noodles, rice vermicelli or rice sticks

1 tablespoon vegetable oil

3 tablespoons chopped dried shrimp

3 tablespoons sliced garlic

3 tablespoons sliced shallots

225 g (8 oz) minced pork

3 tablespoons fish sauce (*nam pla*)

1 tablespoon sugar

3 tablespoons lime juice

3–4 small, fresh red or green Thai chillies, seeded and chopped

salt and freshly ground black pepper to taste

To garnish:

50 g (2 oz) roasted peanuts, crushed

a few fresh coriander sprigs

1 Soak the rice noodles in a bowl of warm water for 25 minutes, then drain them in a colander or sieve.

2 Heat a wok or large frying-pan over a high heat and add the oil. When it is very hot and slightly smoking, add the dried shrimp and garlic and stir-fry for 1 minute, until golden brown. Then add the shallots and pork and stir-fry for 3 minutes.

3 Now add the fish sauce, sugar, lime juice, chillies, salt, pepper and finally the drained noodles. Stir-fry for 3–4 minutes. Turn on to a large platter and sprinkle the garnishes on top. Serve at once, or let it cool and serve at room temperature.

Green bean salad

The Thais enjoy a native vegetable called the winged bean. It is bright green and has a decorative frill on each side, giving it a 'winged' appearance. In this recipe, *yam thua fug yao*, they are blanched and then tossed in an aromatic dressing, making a lovely side dish to serve with curries. If winged beans are not available you could substitute runner beans or French beans.

serves 2–4
preparation time: 15 minutes
cooking time: 3 minutes

450 g (1 lb) winged beans or
    runner beans, sliced if long,
    or French beans

2 small, fresh red or green
    Thai chillies, seeded and
    chopped

2 teaspoons sugar

2 tablespoons lime juice

2 tablespoons fish sauce
    (*nam pla*) or light soy sauce

200 ml (7 fl oz) tinned
    coconut milk

5 tablespoons finely sliced
    shallots

3 tablespoons crushed roasted
    peanuts

2 tablespoons toasted
    desiccated coconut

1 Blanch the beans in a large pan of boiling salted water for 3 minutes, then drain and plunge them immediately into cold water. Drain thoroughly and set aside.

2 Put the chillies, sugar, lime juice, fish sauce or soy sauce and coconut milk in a bowl and mix well.

3 Toss the blanched beans and
shallots with this mixture.
Garnish with the peanuts and
desiccated coconut and serve.

Stir-fried broad beans with red curry

Buttery, succulent broad beans are a favourite throughout Asia. In Thailand they are stir-fried with red curry paste, which gives them a rich and refreshing dimension without masking their distinctive qualities. This dish, called *thua pak-a-phad prig daeng*, makes an impressive and delicious side dish or vegetarian first course. Broad beans are, of course, best eaten as fresh as can be, but frozen beans are a very acceptable substitute (they are usually frozen with the skins already removed).

serves 2–4
preparation time: 25 minutes
cooking time: 5 minutes

900 g (2 lb) fresh broad beans (unshelled weight) or 350 g (12 oz) frozen broad beans

1 tablespoon vegetable oil

3 tablespoons finely sliced garlic

3 tablespoons finely sliced shallots

2 small, fresh red Thai chillies, seeded and sliced

freshly ground black pepper to taste

2 teaspoons sugar

2 teaspoons Thai red curry paste

1 tablespoon fish sauce (*nam pla*) or light soy sauce

2 tablespoons water

1 If you are using fresh broad beans, shell them and then blanch in a large pan of boiling salted water for 2 minutes. Drain thoroughly, refresh in cold water and drain again. When cool, slip off the skins. If you are using frozen beans, simply thaw them.

2 Heat a wok or large frying-pan over a high heat and add the oil. When it is very hot and slightly smoking, add the garlic, shallots, chillies and black pepper and stir-fry for 1 minute.

3 Add the broad beans, sugar, red curry paste, fish sauce and water and continue to stir-fry over a high heat for 2 minutes. Serve at once.

Menus

A Thai meal is a mixture of Thai- and Chinese-influenced dishes, since many people in Thailand are of Chinese extraction. Therefore a typical menu would comprise stir-fried meat, vegetable and noodle dishes with fiery Thai curries, refreshing salads and a variety of dipping sauces.

Here are some suggestions for combining Thai dishes in this book:

Family Dinner

Northern Thai chicken noodle soup
(*khao soi*)

Braised clams with chilli and basil
(*hoy lai phad prik*)

Spicy noodle salad
(*yam woon sen*)

Quick and Easy Meal

Spicy pomelo salad
(*yam som-o*)

Stir-fried minced pork with basil
(*moo phad bai orapa*)

Coconut rice
(*khao mun*)

Authentic Thai Meal

Spicy prawn and lemon grass soup
(*tom yam ghoong*)

Green curry prawns
(*gaeng kheow wan ghoong*)

Crispy fish with mango salad
(*pla samlee thod krob gub yam mamuang*)

Classic Thai fried rice
(*khao phad ruam mit*)

Thai-style Party with Drinks

Thai-style spring rolls
(*poh piah tod*)

Thai fish cakes
(*thod mun pla*)

Crispy corn cakes
(*tod mun khao phod*)

Crispy wontons with sweet chilli sauce
(*kiew grob thai*)

Summer Dinner

Spicy papaya salad
(*som tam*)

Thai barbecue chicken
(*gai yang*)

Coconut mussels
(*hoy malaeng pooh gathi*)

Vegetarian Feast

Savoury rice soup
(*kao tom* – made with vegetable stock)

Stir-fried mixed vegetables
(*phad phag ruam mit*)

Sweet and sour aubergines
(*yam makhua*)

Vegetarian fried rice
(*khao phad jay*)

Thai Street Food

Stir-fried rice noodles
(*phad thai*)

Chicken in pandan leaves
(*gai hor bai* toey)

Hearty Winter Dinner

Coconut chicken soup
(*tom kha gai*)

Mussaman-style beef curry
(*mussaman nuea*)
or Green chicken curry
(*gaeng kheow wan gai*)

Steamed rice

Seafood Lover's Menu

Tasty fried prawns
(*ghoong thod*)

Seafood in coconut milk
(*hor mok talay*)

Fish with chilli sauce
(*chuchi pla nuea orn*)

Steamed rice

Index

Acknowledgements

When Viv Bowler at BBC Books asked me what I wanted to publish next, I suggested returning to basics with *Foolproof Chinese Cookery*. She immediately saw the potential of such a book and asked if I would write one on Thai cooking too. This is the result of her inspiration. So it is natural that I must thank her first.

Gordon Wing faithfully tested each recipe and I thank him for his insight and his excellent suggestions for changes to make the recipes work better.

There is, of course, all the hard-working team at BBC Books who so kindly nurtured this book, including my publisher, Robin Wood; the editor who supervised the book, Sarah Lavelle; the copy editor, Jane Middleton; Viv's efficient assistant, Vicki Vrint; and the most creative and imaginative art director, Lisa Pettibone. To them, I take a deep bow.

I am grateful as well to Jean Cazals for his fluid and imaginative photographs.

And finally, of course, to Carole Blake, my literary agent and friend. An appreciative thanks.